LAST-MINUTE FABRIC GIFTS

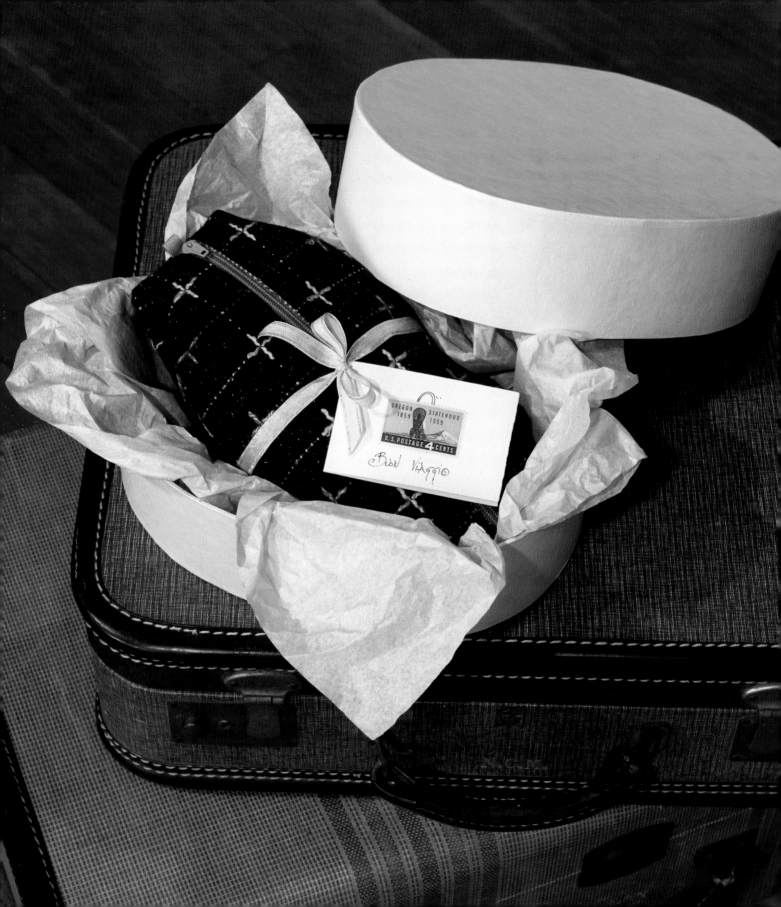

LAST-MINUTE
FABRIC GIFTS

30 HAND-SEW, MACHINE-SEW & NO-SEW PROJECTS

CYNTHIA TREEN

PHOTOGRAPHS BY KAREN PHILIPPI

STC CRAFT | A MELANIE FALICK BOOK
NEW YORK

Editor: Melanie Falick
Designer: Winsor Pop
Production Manager: Kim Tyner

Library of Congress Cataloging-in-Publication Data
Treen, Cynthia.
Last-minute fabric gifts / Cynthia Treen ;
photographs by Karen Philippi.
p. cm.
"A Melanie Falick book."
Includes bibliographical references and index.
ISBN 1-58479-485-2
1. Textile crafts. 2. Sewing. 3. Gifts. I. Title.
TT699.T72 2006
746–dc22
2006001047

Published in 2006 by Stewart, Tabori & Chang
An imprint of Harry N. Abrams, Inc.

The text of this book was composed in Avenir.

Printed and bound in China

10 9 8 7 6 5 4 3 2 1

HNA
harry n. abrams, inc.
a subsidiary of La Martinière Groupe

115 West 18th Street
New York, NY 10011
www.hnabooks.com

To my loving parents, who have always encouraged my creativity.

CONTENTS

INTRODUCTION

When I was asked to write this book on last-minute fabric gifts, I was thrilled because I knew it would allow me to share both my love of working with fabric and one of the secret joys of sewing—immediate gratification. I have long understood that it is possible to pick up a piece of cloth and, within an hour or two, transform it into something wonderful. I can make a skirt in the afternoon and wear it out that evening, or make a new scarf, pillow, bag, or hat and put it to use right away. As a designer working with textiles, I have found that fabric allows for endless invention. In my studio, my eclectic projects range from large-scale sculptures to wedding dresses, draperies, custom bedding, and, of course, last-minute gifts.

The projects in this book embrace this sense of possibility. For many of them, you don't need much sewing experience. There are no-sew, hand-sew, and machine-sew projects to choose from. They are grouped by chapter according to the time it will take most people to complete them comfortably—less than one hour, one to two hours, two to three hours, and three or more hours. In the final chapter, I provide ideas for wrapping gifts when they are finished. To satisfy the visual learner as well as those who prefer to read directions, I have included both detailed illustrations and clear and concise text to guide you through the projects.

When thinking about getting started, remember that fabric is all around you. Consider recycling something, such as an old coat or sweater, or pick up special fabrics when you see them so that you always have the basics on hand. Because fabric selection is limited in some areas, I have included both traditional stores and Internet merchants in the Sources for Supplies on page 140. As you explore the projects in this book, you will learn many of my favorite techniques and will quickly be able to adapt them to express your own unique style. Whether making a gift for a friend or a little something to treat yourself, you can customize color, pattern, and texture to suit the occasion. Just as you would consult a cookbook for techniques and ingredients and then adapt the recipe to your individual taste, you should consider this book a collection of guidelines on which you can easily improvise.

Although the fast pace of our lives can make it hard to find time for handcrafting, I find that taking time to make a gift for a friend or family member is a gift for me as well—just an hour or two of creating with fabric can feel like a small vacation. Rather than spending hours hunting for something in a store, wouldn't you rather spend your time creating at home? I developed these projects with both the beginner and the advanced sewer in mind, so no matter what your schedule or skill level, you can always create a special fabric gift. A patchwork pillow or a warm, luxurious blanket that you have sewn by hand imparts more than fleeting warmth or comfort; it's a lasting token of your esteem and affection. No one need know it was last-minute!

FABRIC BASICS

choosing fabrics

I love to go fabric shopping to see all of the different designs and to compare colors, textures, and weights. While developing the projects for this book, I treated myself to hours of browsing in the many fabric stores in New York City's Garment District. Although it was a wonderful experience, it is not necessary, in most cases, to have the selection that the Garment District offers. Local stores are great resources for a wide range of fabrics, and always have hidden treasures tucked in the shelves. I have also found the Internet to be an excellent resource (especially the many merchants willing to send out sample swatches) and I have included a list of my favorite Internet merchants on page 140. Personally, I like to check out fabrics wherever I go, and buy whatever strikes my fancy so that I have a variety to choose from in my studio whenever I want to start a new project. Other people I know like to shop for fabric after they have decided exactly what they want to make, at which point they know exactly how many yards to buy and can envision the finished piece.

For the projects in this book, I chose fabrics that are both easy and interesting to work with. Advanced sewers may want to substitute other types of fabric; beginners should consider avoiding stretchy, slippery, or velvety fabrics that can be difficult to control. Remember that even the simplest fabric can be made into a beautiful gift. The key is to let the fabric inspire rather than intimidate you. And, most important, have fun with it!

caring for fabric

When buying cloth by the yard, you do not have the advantage of a care label to guide you, and are left to your own devices as far as washing. From my work and washing experience, I know that many clothing companies protect themselves by recommending dry cleaning even when it is not necessary. I do not particularly like to dry-clean because of its effect on the environment and because it is more expensive and time-consuming than machine washing, so I suppose that makes me a more adventurous washer than most. But I have done many wash tests on fabric samples and believe that most of my disasters are behind me.

Following are instructions for how to do a wash test. On page 14 I have provided an overview of the four types of fabric—cotton, linen, wool, and silk—used in the projects in this book, as well as some general guidelines for their care.

WASH TEST

For projects that you would like to be able to machine-wash and machine-dry, I recommend a wash test to see how the fabric will respond. If this is not important to you, you can simply hand-wash and line-dry the item, or dry-clean it.

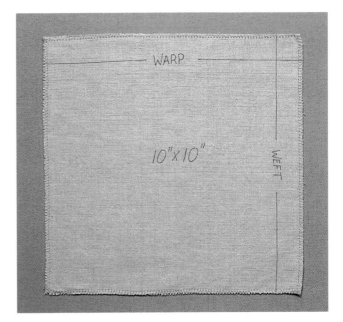

To do a wash test, cut a 10" square of fabric and make a zigzag stitch around the edges so they will not fray. With a permanent pen, label the warp (length) and weft (width). Machine-wash and tumble dry the square using the machine settings you prefer so you can find out if you will be able to wash the finished project with your other laundry. If you like the result of the wash test, wash and dry the entire piece of fabric on the same settings before you cut and sew the project. If your 10" square shrinks considerably, then you should estimate what you will lose in shrinkage and add that amount to its length before washing. (For example, if the warp of the 10" square shrinks to 8", then one yard or 36" of the same fabric will shrink approximately 6" to 8" in length.)

fiber types

COTTON

Cotton comes from the boll of the cotton plant. It is soft, durable, absorbent, and usually requires little in terms of special care. Its fibers vary in length—the longer the fiber, the higher the quality of fabric. You may want to prewash and tumble dry cotton fabric to preshrink it and/ or remove any sizing (a surface treatment applied by the manufacturer to stiffen and finish fabric). In most cases, woven cottons tend not to slip or stretch much during sewing and press well, but different weaves may vary.

LINEN

Linen is made from the fibers inside the stem of the flax plant, and is the earliest known fiber to be woven into cloth. Its use dates back thousands of years to ancient Egypt, where traces of shrouds have been found at burial sites. Linen is one of my favorite fabrics for home decorating and for cool summer clothing. It is durable, elegant, and breathes well.

Linen can be crisp or quite soft, depending on how it is finished. Damasks and fabric intended for table linens can sometimes have a glazed finish that enhances the linen's natural sheen. These surface treatments generally wash out, but can be preserved with dry cleaning. How you wear and care for your linen is up to you. Whether you want a crisp look or a softer, wrinkled look, here are a few suggestions for linen care:

Colored linen tends to fade when machine-washed and dried on a warm or hot setting, so I recommend either hand washing cold and line drying, or machine washing cold on a gentle cycle and line drying.

Natural and white linens tend not to fade; items made from them can be machine-washed and dried on a warm setting as long as the fabric was preshrunk by prewashing and drying before the item was made.

Linen has a soft, natural beauty and relaxed look that requires no ironing when it is promptly removed from the dryer. Hand-washed and line-dried linen will also soften after a few washes. If you want a crisp, pressed look without wrinkles, try this trick: Wet the linen and squeeze out any excess water. Fold it, put it in a plastic bag, and place it in the refrigerator for several hours or overnight to chill thoroughly, then take it out and iron immediately. The cool temperature combined with the hot iron makes the wrinkles come out more easily than with steam or spray alone. You can also use ice water in your spray bottle to achieve a similar effect. To restore a crisp look to old linen, use a spray starch when you iron.

WOOL

Strictly speaking, wool is the fiber derived from the fleece of sheep. However, the term "wool" is often used to refer to fabrics made from the fleece of other animals, such as angora and cashmere goats, alpacas, and camels, whose hairs are characterized by tiny scales that bond together and felt. Each of these fibers has its own unique characteristics, making wool a very versatile material. Wool can be light, fluffy, smooth, soft, or dense, depending on how it is knit, woven, or felted. It is warm, resilient, and dyes beautifully, creating fabrics rich in color. Most woven wools are a delight to work with— they are not too slippery, and because of their ability to stretch without becoming too elastic, they are forgiving whether you are sewing by hand or machine.

There are a few options when it comes to washing wool, depending on the outcome you are looking for. Hand washing cold and line drying (for wovens) or flat drying (for knits) are the safest routes for keeping the original look of the fabric. Sometimes, though, you may want to change the hand of the fabric altogether by intentionally shrinking it. It is liberating to throw wool in the washer and dryer and watch the fibers shrink and felt, yielding denser fabric with edges that can be cut without fraying or unraveling.

SILK

Silk is produced by silkworms and is one of the finest fibers found in nature. Silk fabric comes in all sorts of weights and weaves, giving the fabric many different personalities. It can range from the finest gossamer chiffon to a thick, double-sided silk satin. Depending on the weave, silk fabric can be stretchy, as with crepe, or have no stretch at all, as with taffeta. You may find it helpful to hand-baste your seams rather than pinning them if you are working with a slippery or delicate silk. I hand-wash most of my silks in cold water and line-dry them, but dry cleaning is the only way to preserve the original crisp finish of silk taffeta. Because of the delicate nature of silk, I do not prewash unless I have a specific reason to do so. Beware—silk will shrink and lose its luster if it is washed in warm water, and white silk will turn yellow if bleached.

fabric terms

Here are the most common terms you are likely to encounter when investigating different fabrics:

Appliqué The decorative application of cut pieces of fabric to another base fabric.

Bark cloth This native Polynesian fabric, also called "tapa," was originally made from the soft inner bark of mulberry trees, and was beaten, not woven. It was typically decorated with large bold patterns and worn by Polynesian tribes. The original cloth inspired a cotton version, which is widely used today for upholstery and home decoration.

Bias/true bias A line running at a 45-degree angle to the warp or weft of a piece of fabric is on the true bias. Strips of fabric cut on this angle can be used for binding edges, making narrow fabric tubing, and various other trimming applications. For more on bias, see page 131.

Blend A fabric in which the threads are made up of two or more fibers twisted (or blended) together.

Bouclé A fabric woven with a bouclé yarn. Bouclé yarn is curly in texture and creates a heavily textured surface of loops and slubs when woven.

Brushed A fabric on which the surface fibers have been lifted to create a fuzzy nap. Flannel is an example of a fabric that has a brushed surface.

Buckram A plain weave cotton fabric heavily stiffened with sizing or glue, commonly used in drapery-making and bookbinding.

Canvas A heavyweight, durable, plain weave cotton.

Chambray A lightweight, plain weave cotton that has a colored warp and a white weft, creating a slightly iridescent appearance.

Charmeuse A silk fabric with a satin surface and a flowing drape.

Chenille A fabric that is woven from yarn of the same name. The yarn and the fabric have a plush, velvety surface. The short hairs of the yarn stick out from a twisted central cord.

Corduroy A fabric (typically cotton) that has a cordlike cut-pile surface.

Cotton The soft, fluffy fiber harvested from the seedpod, or boll, of the cotton plant. The longer the cotton fibers, the higher quality the fabric. Of all the cotton varieties, pima and Egyptian cotton have the longest fibers and are known for the excellent quality of fabric that can be made from them.

Crepe A fabric with a slightly crinkled surface, such as wool crepe and crepe georgette.

Denim A tight twill weave cotton fabric in which the warp threads are colored (typically indigo) and the weft threads are not dyed. Because of the twill weave, the surface of the fabric takes on the color of the warp threads.

Double-faced A fabric with no wrong side, usable on both sides.

Drape The fall of the fabric, the way it hangs.

Dupioni A plain weave silk fabric with a slubbed, irregular surface that has a crisp hand similar to taffeta.

Flannel A plain weave cotton fabric that has either one or both of its surfaces brushed after weaving to lift up fibers and create a plush, fuzzy finish.

Gabardine A wool fabric with a tight twill weave typically used today for suiting.

Gauze A lightweight, sheer fabric with a plain open weave.

Gingham   A fabric, usually cotton, with an even plaid that forms a checkerboard pattern.

Grain   The direction of the fibers in a woven fabric.

Grosgrain   A fabric made with a warp of fine threads and a weft of thin cords, producing a ribbed surface. This fabric is usually turned into ribbon or given a special treatment to create moiré.

Hand   The feel of a fabric in the hand (for example, a stiff, supple, or velvety hand).

Heather   A fabric woven with multicolored threads spun together to create a slightly speckled, or heathered, appearance on the fabric's surface.

Jacquard   A fabric woven on a loom of the same name and characterized by its intricately patterned surfaces, as in damasks and brocades.

Jersey   A small-gauge, machine-knit fabric without any ribbing that has a distinct right and wrong side.

Linen   A fabric made from the fibers harvested from the stem of the flax plant.

Mercerization   A process used to swell the fibers of cotton threads or yarns to increase strength, sheen, and dye receptivity.

Moiré   Grosgrain fabric pressed with engraved rollers to create a wavy, waterlike pattern.

Muslin   A light- to medium-weight, natural-colored plain weave cotton.

Nap   The surface texture of a fabric. Velvet, corduroy, and flannel have a directional nap (meaning the threads all want to lay in the same direction).

Organdy A sheer, stiff, plain weave fabric typically made from cotton.

Organza A sheer silk with a stiff, starchy hand, usually a plain weave but also occasionally made with a satin weave.

Plain weave A weave in which the warp and weft alternate going over and under one another to create a fabric with tight structure.

Pongee A Chinese or Indian plain weave silk with a soft hand, typically in a natural, unbleached color (can be thought of as a silk version of muslin).

Satin A weave of fabric in which the weft threads are floated over a few warp threads at a time to create a smooth, even, lustrous surface.

Selvage The tightly woven edge (usually a plain weave) that stops fabric from fraying.

Shantung A silk with a slubbed texture similar to dupioni, but with a duller surface.

Silk chiffon A very lightweight, plain weave silk fabric that is sheer like organza and has a fluid drape like charmeuse.

Silk satin A generic term for any silk fabric woven with a satin weave.

Silk georgette A very lightweight, sheer, plain weave silk that has a fluid drape and a slightly crinkled or crepe surface.

Silk taffeta A plain weave silk fabric that has a crisp hand and a lustrous matte surface. A skirt made from silk taffeta can sound like rustling leaves when it moves.

Size A glaze or surface treatment used to stiffen and finish fabrics. It is usually made from glue, wax, or clay, and can be washed out.

Terry A knit or woven fabric (usually cotton) that is characterized by a looped surface. The loops can be either cut or uncut, and on one or both sides of the fabric.

Thread count The number of warp and weft threads in one square inch of fabric.

Ticking A tightly woven striped twill or plain weave cotton fabric traditionally used for mattress and pillow covers. The term has come to mean any striped fabric resembling that style.

Tweed A twill weave fabric (usually wool) woven with a yarn containing many different-colored slubs.

Twill A woven fabric with stepped floats (areas where weft threads are carried over a few warp threads at a time) forming a diagonal pattern on its surface.

Velvet A soft, lustrous, cut-pile fabric traditionally woven in silk, but now more commonly woven with a silk crepe back and a rayon pile.

Voile A lightweight, tight, plain weave cotton with a cloudy appearance and a slightly crisp hand.

Warp The threads that run the length of the fabric (perpendicular to the weft).

Weft The threads that run the width of the fabric (perpendicular to the warp).

LESS-THAN-ONE-HOUR GIFTS

bias blossom *Hand-sew*

With its ruffled edges and its fluffy stamen, this blossom reminds me of a tree peony. It can be made into a brooch, a hair ornament, a package decoration, or—in a smaller size—an embellishment for the Felted Silk Scarf on page 80. I have made these blossoms in many different kinds of silk, including iridescent taffeta, organza, chiffon, and lining silk. I am sure they would also look wonderful in a cotton voile or tissue linen.

MATERIALS

4" × 36" strip bias (see page 131)

1½" square piece felt

Thread to match

1 skein cotton or silk embroidery floss, for stamen

3"–5" doll needle

Hand-sewing needle

Embroidery needle

2" safety pin or small barrette

Water-erasable pen

Stiffen Stuff spray stiffener (optional)

Fabri-Tac adhesive

Note: To create a fuller flower, start with a bias strip longer than 36".

1 With a water-erasable pen, mark a line down the 36" length of the center of the bias strip. Hand-sew a running stitch (approximately ¼" stitch length) down the centerline of the bias strip.

2 Pull the thread so it gathers the bias tightly. At the end of your gathered stitch line, make a few tacking stitches to secure the end of the thread, but do not cut the thread (you will use it to wrap the fabric into a bundle).

3 To create the bundle, tightly roll up the gathered bias strip, starting at the end where you began your running stitch. (This tightly rolled center gives the flower its structural integrity.) Hold one side of the bundle in your hand to keep the ruffles out of the way and, with your other hand, wrap the thread tail around the bundle several times. Secure the thread by making a few tacking stitches through the wrapped area, then knot off and cut the thread.

4 With the eye end of the doll needle, skewer through the center of the roll you just made and set aside.

5 Make a small tassel for the stamen: Cut 1 yard embroidery floss. Wrap the floss around your index finger 15 to 20 times, then cut off the end and set aside the remainder (about 10" to 12"). Without letting it unwind, pull the wrapped floss off your finger and keep it in a coil shape. Thread the leftover floss through the center of the coil and tie a knot, leaving equal amounts of floss on both sides. This will keep the coil in place and prevent it from unwinding. Cut through the loop of floss opposite the knot to create a tassel.

Steps 1–4

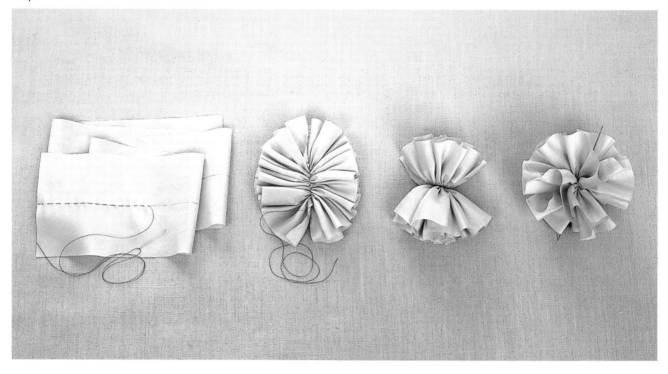

Steps 5–8

6   If desired, press the flower flat to make it easier to see what you are doing. To attach the tassel/stamen to the flower, thread both ends of the tassel tie onto the eye of the doll needle and pull it through the center of the flower. Remove the doll needle and continue to pull the tassel ties until the knotted end of the tassel appears on the other side of the flower. Separate the two ties, thread one of the ties onto an embroidery needle, and make a stitch through the back of the flower. Remove the needle and make a double knot with the two ties. Trim the fringe of the tassel/stamen on the front of the flower as desired.

7   Evenly dampen the flower with water. Scrunch up the petals and rub them back and forth against the palm of your hand to fringe the edges of the bias and create a soft, wrinkled texture. Work and sculpt the petals until you achieve the look you want. If the center petals are too long, trim them back as desired. Then set aside to dry. If you are using a very lightweight fabric, you may also want to use a spray stiffener such as Stiffen Stuff to stiffen and shape the petals. Spray the Stiffen Stuff on the petals and sculpt them with your fingers.

8   When the flower has dried, open the pin or barrette and lay it on the center back of the flower. Spread an even layer of Fabri-Tac on one side of the felt piece. Lay the felt, sticky side down, on the back of the flower, sandwiching the back side of the pin or barrette between the felt and the flower. Leave the point of the pin or arm of the barrette free to open and close. Set aside to dry.

coat sleeve bag *Hand-sew*

I met Stacy Cristo a few years ago and fell in love with the bags she was making from recycled clothing. She made this one from the sleeve of a coat. Once you get the hang of it, it only takes about 30 minutes to complete.

MATERIALS

Coat with lined sleeves (overcoats and blazers work well as long as they're not super-thick)

Thread to match

Hand-sewing needle

Iron and ironing board

Fabri-Tac

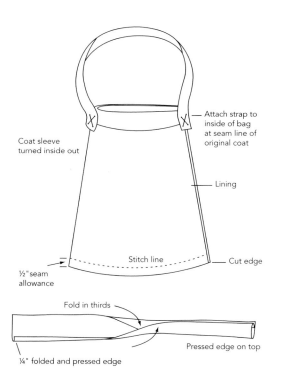

Coat sleeve turned inside out

Attach strap to inside of bag at seam line of original coat

Lining

½" seam allowance

Stitch line

Cut edge

Fold in thirds

Pressed edge on top

¼" folded and pressed edge

Strap cut on straight grain

1 Cut off one sleeve about 10½" from the cuff edge. (You may want to vary this measurement depending on the proportion of the sleeve you are using.) Turn the sleeve inside out. With a ½" seam allowance and a running stitch, sew the cut end closed, making a few backstitches along the stitch line to strengthen the seam. At the end of your seam, make a few tacking stitches to secure the end of your thread, then knot it off.

2 The strap on the bag shown here came from the belt of the original coat. If you do not have this detail on your coat, make a strap from some of the leftover fabric. To make the strap, cut a 3" × 22" strip of fabric from the body of the coat, cutting on the straight grain. Make the strap length proportional to the size of your bag. Fold and press one of the long edges under ¼". Fold the length of the fabric strip in thirds, with the pressed edge on top so the pressed edge covers and encloses the opposite cut edge. Secure the fold with a thin line of Fabri-Tac or stitch the seam by hand using a fell stitch. Fold the strap ends about ½" and secure the fold with a thin line of Fabri-Tac (or stitch the fold by hand using a fell stitch).

3 Pin the strap ends to the inside of the bag at the seam lines. Make several cross-shaped stitches to attach them; repeat several times in the same place to secure the strap. Turn the bag right side out.

tie pouch *Hand-sew*

This is another of my friend Stacy Cristo's wonderful recycled bags. She has a great imagination and breathes new life and function into simple, everyday fabrics. This pouch can be made from all types of neckties, and the ties you choose can dictate what type of pouch you make. Try using a solid-colored silk tie to create an elegant evening bag (you can also add beaded handles), or use a more casual tie for a playful makeup bag.

MATERIALS

Necktie (wide-bottomed ties are great for larger bags; narrow ties make nice jewelry storage bags)

Thread in contrasting color

Hand-sewing needle

½ yard ⅜"-wide twill tape

Coat-hook decorative fastener

Iron and ironing board

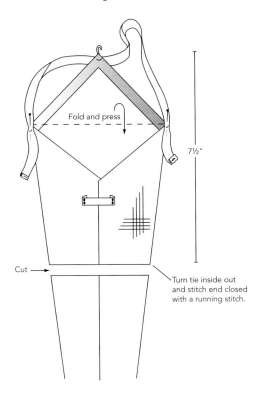

1 Cut off the end of the tie about 7½" from the point. Some ties are not stitched up the center seam in the back. If this is the case with yours, close up the seam with a fell stitch; if not, just turn the tie inside out.

2 With a ½" seam allowance and a running stitch, sew the cut end closed, making a few backstitches along the stitch line to strengthen the seam. At the end of your seam, make a few tacking stitches to secure the end of your thread, then knot it off.

3 Turn the tie right side out and press the bottom seam flat. Press the point down to create an envelope flap.

4 Cut a 12" piece of twill tape. Pin the ends to the pouch at the corners where the flap folds down, leaving a 2" tail at each corner. Attach the tape to the bag at the two pin points using several small tacking stitches on top of one another (as though you were attaching a button). Knot off your thread inside the bag. Roll the ends of the 2" tails and make a few tacking stitches to finish the ends.

5 Stitch the hook to the point of the envelope flap so the hooked end hangs off the point of the tie.

6 Cut a 2" piece of twill tape for the hook to loop through. Fold the envelope flap down to determine where the tape loop should be attached. Place the tape so its bottom edge is even with the bottom of the hook and the loop is centered on the pouch. Pin it in place. Fold under the ends of the tape, then attach the loop using the same button-style tacking stitch. When you finish tacking the tape ends in place, bring your needle and thread to the inside of the pouch to hide your finishing knots.

corduroy change purse *Machine-sew*

For this little change purse, choose a light- to medium-weight durable fabric that will hold up to change knocking against it. I like to use corduroy because it comes in bright, fun colors and narrow- to wide-wale sizes. I cut the wale in a different direction for each purse to make each one slightly unique.

MATERIALS

One 5" × 5" and one 2" × 5" piece cotton corduroy

7" polyester, all-purpose zipper, in contrasting color

Thread to match fabric

Fray Check (optional)

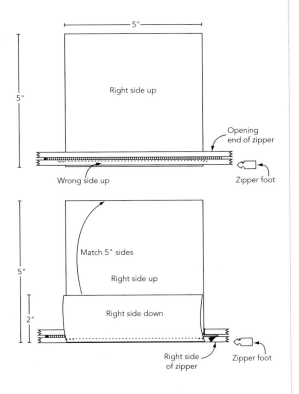

1   Lay the zipper, closed and with the back side facing up, along one of the 5" sides of the square corduroy piece. The zipper ends will overhang the edges of the fabric by about 1". Match the zipper tape edge and the fabric edge to one another and pin the zipper in place.

2   Using a zipper foot, stitch along the zipper tape with the side of the foot resting against the teeth as you stitch (³⁄₈" seam allowance). Because of the zipper's extra length, the zipper pull should be out of your way the entire time you are sewing, so there is no need to open and close the zipper as you sew.

3   Splay the zipper and the fabric open so that their right sides are facing up. Lay the 5" edge of the rectangular piece of fabric, with the right side facing down, onto the unsewn side of the zipper tape. Pin the fabric to the zipper tape, matching the edges.

4   Using the zipper foot, stitch along the fabric edge with the zipper facing up under the fabric and the side of the foot resting against the teeth as you stitch.

5   Splay the fabric open to expose the zipper and press flat. Unzip the zipper partway so you will be able to turn the change purse after the front and back are stitched together.

6   With right sides together, match the two 5" ends that are parallel to the zipper and pin them together. Sew around the three cut sides with a ½" seam allowance, backstitching over both ends of the zipper as well as the beginning and end of your stitch line. Trim off the overhanging zipper ends so they are flush with the fabric edge. Trim the corners at a 45-degree angle.

7   Because the seam allowances are likely to fray from the change moving around inside, secure the fibers by either making a zigzag stitch on the seam allowances or by applying a fabric adhesive (like Fray Check) to them. Turn the purse right side out and press, if necessary.

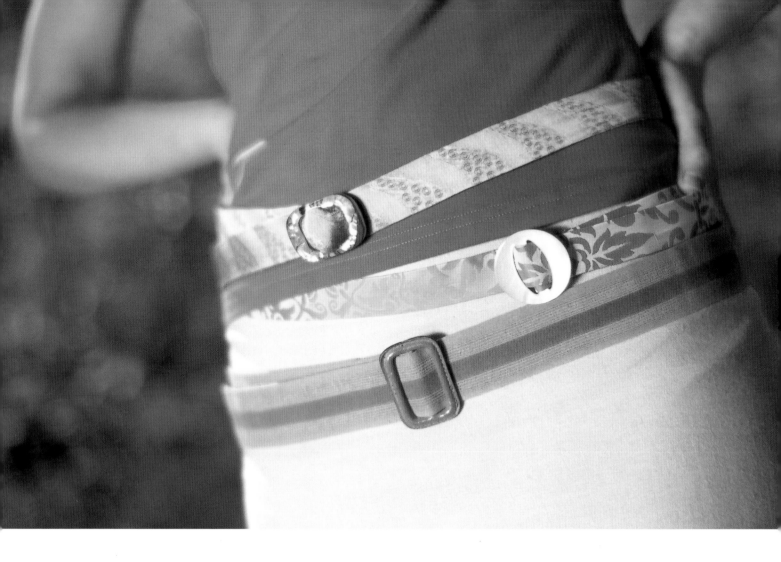

fabric belt *Hand-sew*

A patterned fabric belt can be a colorful complement to any outfit, and is as simple to make as it is to wear. The length of the belt comes from the width of the fabric you choose; 54"-wide fabric should be long enough for most belts. If the fabric width happens to be narrower than the length of the belt you want to make, connect two pieces of fabric together. I've used silk brocade, cotton, and linen to make belts. Most woven fabrics will work well; knits and very thick fabrics will not.

MATERIALS

4" × 58" piece woven fabric

Banroll (or other stiffening material), as wide as buckle's center bar and 56" long (see Note)

Thread to match

Hand-sewing needle

Slide buckle

Iron and ironing board

Fabri-Tac adhesive (optional)

Note: There are several materials that can be used for stiffening belts. I use Banroll, which is a stiff, narrowly woven fabric that has flexibility primarily in its length, making it ideal for this use (it is used to keep waistbands from curling). It comes in a variety of widths to fit various buckle sizes but it can be trimmed down to width, if necessary. Its width should be equal to the interior dimension of the buckle you have chosen.

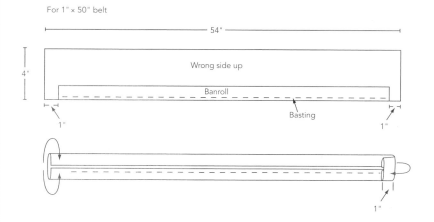

For 1" × 50" belt

1. Lay the fabric wrong side up on your work surface. Lay the Banroll on top of the fabric, matching one of its long edges to one of the fabric's long edges. Center the Banroll along that edge so 1" of fabric extends beyond either end. Pin the Banroll in place, then baste to the fabric with large stitches.

2. Fold the two long sides in so they meet in the center (the Banroll should be inside the fold closest to you). Press flat. Fold one of the fabric ends in so it is snug against the end of the Banroll. Press it flat. Fold the length of the belt in half and press it flat.

3. Use a fell stitch to sew the long side and the folded end closed. Fold the remaining end under and stitch in place (or use Fabri-Tac adhesive).

4. Slip the end you have just stitched (or glued) through the center of the belt buckle so the belt catches and loops around the center bar. Pull about 2" of the belt through the buckle, then fold back the end of the belt. Pin it to the back side of the belt, and sew in place with a fell stitch.

fabric envelopes *No-sew*

Just like the Fabric-Covered Notebook on page 40, these handsome envelopes are made by backing fabric with paper. For an extra-special touch, make a paper sleeve, seal it with a Velcro dot, or tie it with ribbon. I've included measurements for three sizes: One for a wedding or graduation card that holds money, one for a CD, and one that fits a greeting card you can make by folding an 8½" × 11" sheet of paper into quarters (4¼" × 5½")—but you can make these envelopes as large or as small as you need. Avoid very lacy fabric because the adhesive will seep through, and very thick fabric because it does not fold as well.

MATERIALS
(to make any of the three suggested sizes)

15" × 8" piece silk or cotton
(not too lacy or thick)

15" × 8" piece Steam-A-Seam 2
Double Stick Fusible Web

15" × 8" piece paper, roughly
the weight of computer paper (20lb.)

Rotary cutter and cutting mat

Clear plastic ruler

Iron, ironing board, and press cloth

Tacky Glue

Bone folder

Narrow ribbon, Velcro dots,
or additional paper for sleeve (optional)

1 Lay the fabric, wrong side up, on the rotary cutting mat. Peel the paper backing off one side of the Steam-A-Seam and lay it, sticky side down, onto the fabric. With the rotary cutter and ruler, trim the fabric and Steam-A-Seam together to the envelope size of your choice (money card: 7" × 7", CD case: 13" × 5½", or greeting card: 12½" × 6½"). Remove the paper backing from the other side of the Steam-A-Seam.

2 Place your paper, wrong side up, onto the cutting mat. With the fabric facing up, roughly center the Steam-A-Seam and fabric on top of the paper. Make sure you have at least ¼" paper overhang all the way around the fabric.

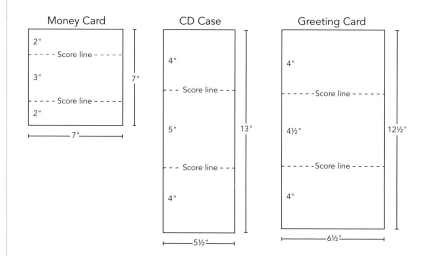

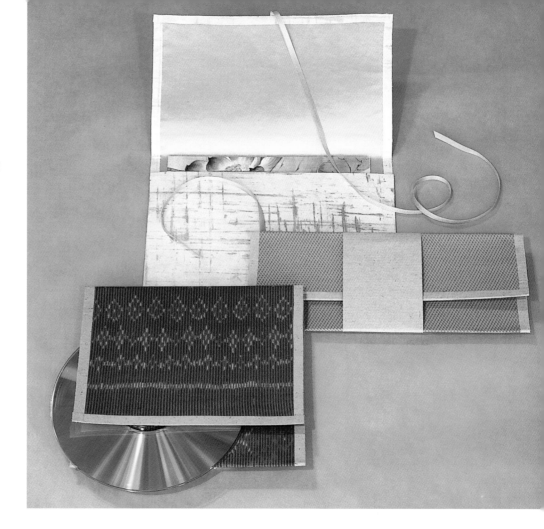

3 Transfer the fabric, web, and paper sandwich to the ironing board. Place a press cloth on top and press in 10- to 20-second increments until the fabric and paper are fused together (do not exceed 60 seconds total).

4 Lay the sandwich, fabric side up, on the rotary cutting mat. Using the rotary cutter and the ruler, trim the paper edges to a ¼" overhang all the way around. With the fabric side up, spread a thin layer of Tacky Glue on the ¼" paper overhang. Fold the paper edges over on all sides to enclose the raw edge of the fabric.

5 Decide whether you want to have the fabric or the paper on the outside of the envelope. Place the outside face down on your work surface. Using a bone folder and the ruler, score lines parallel to both short ends of the pieces to create the fold lines of the pocket and the flap (money card: 2" from each end, CD case: 4" from each end, or greeting card: 4" from each end). Place a thin line of glue on the left and right edges of the envelope, from the bottom score line to the corner. Fold the bottom section up at the score line to seal the sides, creating the pocket of the envelope. Fold the top section down at the score line to create the flap of the envelope. Press the envelope flat.

6 If you want, add a paper sleeve by cutting a narrow strip of paper long enough to wrap around the belly of the envelope. Wrap it around the envelope and glue it closed where the paper overlaps. You can also glue a Velcro dot in place to close the envelope, or tie it up with a delicate ribbon, if desired.

felt rabbits *Hand-sew*

These rabbits can hop around the Garden Play Mat (page 102), or one can be a little gift all by itself. If you do not have time to make both a rabbit and the mat, make a rabbit first, then make the mat to give at a later date.

MATERIALS

Tracing paper, for pattern

5" × 5" piece wool felt

Thread to match felt

Black thread, for eyes

Tan embroidery floss

Hand-sewing needle

1 small handful polyfill stuffing

1 Trace the rabbit pattern pieces on page 38, cut them out, and use them to cut 2 body pieces, 2 ears, 1 tail, and 1 base from the wool felt.

2 To make the body, place one of the cut body pieces over the other, lining up the edges. Using the matching thread, whipstitch up one side, over the curve, and down the other side, leaving the flat bottom open.

3 Place the sewn body on one of your fingers like a finger puppet. Drench the wool with warm water and squeeze out the excess moisture with a towel while the body is still on your finger. This will give it a more three-dimensional form and make the whipstitch seam less visible.

4 Remove the body from your finger and pack it tightly with stuffing (don't worry if the wool is slightly damp; it will finish drying as you work). Take the circle of wool for the base of the rabbit and place it over the bottom hole. Holding it in place, whipstitch around its circumference to close the hole.

5 To form the neck, make one big stitch from side seam to side seam, about one-third of the way down from the rounded top of the head. Draw the stitch in tightly, stitching over it a few times before you knot off your thread.

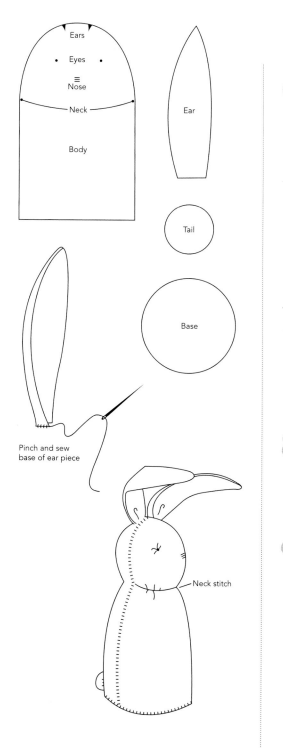

Ears

• Eyes •

≡
Nose

Neck

Body

Ear

Tail

Base

Pinch and sew
base of ear piece

Neck stitch

6   To make the eyes, thread the needle with black thread and knot the end. Insert your needle into the side of the face, about halfway between the neckline (created by the stitch in Step 5) and the top of the head. Pull it through to the other side of the face to mark the second eye. Stitch back and forth through the inside of the head, making two separate eyes. Keep the thread tight as you sew to cinch the head and create facial contours. When you are finished with the eyes, hide the end of your black thread by inserting the needle one last time into one of the eyes and pulling it out somewhere on the body. Trim the thread close to the body, then pull the wool out where the thread is visible to make it disappear back into the body.

7   To make the ears, pinch and fold the base of the ear piece in half with your fingers. Using matching thread, make a few whipstitches along the folded base to secure the fold and create a contoured ear base. Repeat for the other ear piece. Whipstitch the ear bases, one at a time, to the top of the rabbit's head and knot off your thread.

8   To form the nose, thread the needle with two strands of tan embroidery floss separated from the skein. In the center of the face and slightly below the eyes, make a few tacking stitches on top of each other to form a nose. Hide the end of the thread in the same way as for the eyes.

9   To form the tail, make a running stitch around the circumference of the wool tail piece as close to the edge as possible, cinching the thread so that the round piece forms a small ball. If necessary, secure the ball in place by crossing several more stitches over the gathered opening. Stitch the gathered side of the tail onto the backside of the rabbit just above the base. Use several whipstitches around the ball to attach it to the body, then knot off your thread.

fabric-covered notebook _No-sew_

A fabric-covered notebook is the perfect gift for just about anyone, whether they like to draw, write, or just keep notes. It is made using the same technique as the Fabric Envelopes (page 34).

MATERIALS

9" × 12" (or desired size) pad

⅓ yard linen (more for a larger pad)

1 yard Steam-A-Seam 2 Double Stick Fusible Web

1 roll kraft paper

Tacky Glue

Clear plastic ruler

Rotary cutter and cutting mat

Iron, ironing board, and press cloth

Ribbon, for ties (optional)

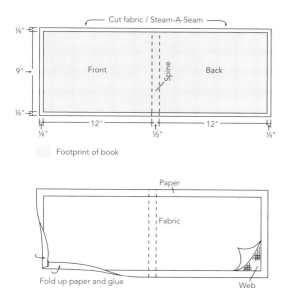

Footprint of book

Fold up paper and glue

1. Remove the front cover of the pad, leaving the back cover on. Orient the pad so the spine is on the left-hand side. The new cover you are making will wrap around the front, spine, and back of the pad and will overhang the page edges by ⅛".

2. To get the footprint size of the notebook, measure the total width for the new cover. For a 9" × 12" pad, add 12" (front width), ½" (spine width), 12" (back width) and ¼" (⅛" overhang for each end) for a total of 24¾". Next, measure the height of the pad, adding the overhang. For a 9" × 12" pad, add 9" (height) and ¼" (⅛" overhang at top and bottom) for a total of 9¼".

3. Cut one 24¾" × 9¼" piece Steam-A-Seam. Peel the paper backing off of one side and lay it, sticky side down, on the back side of the linen. Cut the linen to size with the rotary cutter, using the edges of the Steam-A-Seam as a guide.

4. Cut one piece of kraft paper so you have at least 1" of overhang on all sides of the linen piece (26¾" × 11¼" for a 9" × 12" sketch pad). Remove the paper backing from the other side of the Steam-A-Seam and lay it, sticky side down, on top of the kraft paper, centering it as best you can.

5. Lay the sandwich, fabric side up, on the ironing board. Place a press cloth on top and press in 10- to 20-second increments (do not exceed 60 seconds total).

6. With your rotary cutter and ruler, measure and trim the kraft paper so that it overhangs by ¼" all the way around the fabric.

7. With the fabric side up, spread a thin layer of Tacky Glue on the paper overhang. Fold the paper edges over on all sides to enclose the raw edge of the fabric.

8 Cut one piece Steam-A-Seam the same size as the back of the pad. Remove both sides of the backing and lay the Steam-A-Seam on the back of the pad.

9 To attach the cover to the notebook, place the fabric cover horizontally, paper side up, on your work surface. Center the back of the pad on the right-hand side of the cover, leaving a ⅛" overhang on the top, right, and bottom sides. Flip the book over so the fabric side of the cover is facing up. Lay it on your ironing board, cover with the press cloth, and press the new cover to the back side of the pad. Flip the book over and press the new cover over the front pages, creasing the spine.

10 If you want to add ribbon ties, use Tacky Glue to attach the ribbons to the inside of the front and back covers. Hide the ribbon ends with a small square of paper and glue or Steam-A-Seam it in place.

quick dish towel *Machine-sew*

The idea for this project originated with some friends of mine, when they had just arrived home from the hospital with their new daughter and were also in the process of renovating their kitchen and dining room. Tired and slightly frazzled, they joked that their idea of a last-minute gift was something that could be made in five minutes, in the bathroom, with the person who was to receive it in the next room! With their new baby and kitchen in mind, I came up with this idea for a quick dish towel that might double nicely as a snappy burp cloth. The circular cutout serves as a practical way to hang the towel and a graphic and colorful detail. I like to use large table napkins to make the towels because they are inexpensive, easy to find, and come in a wide variety of vibrant colors.

MATERIALS

20" × 20" solid-colored cotton
or linen napkin

3½" × 3½" piece linen or cotton
(cut from a napkin in a contrasting color)

Thread to match

Compass or circle template with 1" hole

Fabric-marking pencil

Trimming scissors

Iron and ironing board

1 Set the compass to a ½" radius. Place the point of the compass in the center of the 3½"-square of fabric and, with the compass and the fabric-marking pencil, draw a 1" circle. This can also be achieved using a circle template with a 1" hole.

2 Lay the napkin, wrong side up, on your work surface. Place the 3½"-square of fabric on top of the napkin, with the drawn circle side up. Match the edges of the square to the inside of the napkin's hem and pin in place.

3 With your smallest stitch length (#1 stitch on most machines), stitch twice around the circle you drew. To achieve a smooth curve, make only a few stitches at a time, then, with the needle down in the fabric, lift the foot and pivot the work slightly. Keep stitching and pivoting until you have stitched twice around the circle. The seam allowance will be cut very close to your stitch; the double stitch and the small stitch length give the seam line extra strength.

4 Cut out the center of the circle, cutting through both pieces of fabric. Leave a ⅛" seam allowance around the inside of the hole.

5 Push the small square through the hole to the other side of the fabric. Spray the square with water and press flat. Fold the four cut edges of the small square under until they reach the interior seam line of the circle (about ¾"), pressing each edge flat as you go.

6 Topstitch the square as close to the folded edges as possible, or hand-stitch the edges with a fell stitch. Backstitch or knot off your thread as you complete the square.

bark cloth baby bib *Machine-sew*

Bark cloth is typically used for home furnishings, but because of its bright, bold prints and durability, I think it's a wonderful choice for this special baby bib.

MATERIALS

9½" × 12½" piece tracing paper, for pattern

½ yard cotton bark cloth, washed

Two pieces 15" × ¼" twill tape, for ties

Thread to match

Compass

Iron and ironing board

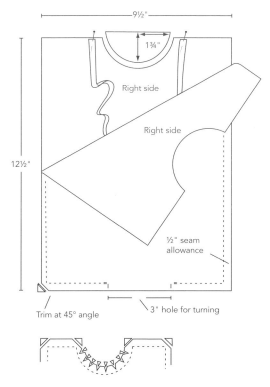

9½"

1¾"

Right side

Right side

12½"

½" seam allowance

Trim at 45° angle

3" hole for turning

Clip corners and notch neckline to reduce bulk

1 To mark the neckline of the bib on your pattern, set the compass so that it has a 1¾" radius. Mark the center point of one of the 9½" sides of your tracing paper. Place the point of the compass on the center point of the tracing paper's edge and, with the compass, draw a 3½" semicircle. Cut along this curved line to create the neckline.

2 Place the fabric, right side up, on a work surface. Pin the tracing paper bib pattern on top of the fabric, making sure you are pleased with where the bark cloth's graphics fall. Cut out a bib front and back, cutting each piece separately to get the best graphics on both sides.

3 Lay one side of the bark cloth, right side up, on your work surface. Pin one end of each twill tape ½" to the right and left of the neckline so the twill tape lies on top of the fabric.

4 Lay the other piece of bark cloth down on top of the first so the right sides are together and the ties are sandwiched between the two pieces. Match the edges of the fabric and pin the front and back together, making sure the ties catch at the neckline. Begin stitching on the bottom side of the bib. With a ½" seam allowance, stitch around the bib, making sure to catch the ties at the neckline. Backstitch at the beginning and the end of your stitchline and leave a 3" hole for turning on the bottom edge of the bib.

5 Before turning, notch the inner curve of the neckline and trim each corner at a 45-degree angle to reduce bulk. Turn the bib right side out. Press the bib, then slipstitch the opening closed.

cat toy *Machine-sew*

Your favorite felines (and their people) will love these colorful toys. Whether you suspend them from homemade fabric spaghetti (see Creating Bias Tubes on page 133) or store-bought ribbon, they are a very quick gift. Be sure to choose strong wool that will hold up to the cat's playfulness.

MATERIALS

Two 3" × 3" pieces brightly colored, dense, sturdy wool

1 yard narrow ribbon or bias tubing, for cord

Catnip teabag (available at pet stores)

Thread to match

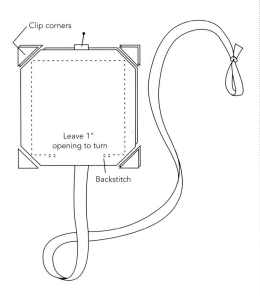

Clip corners

Leave 1" opening to turn

Backstitch

1   Place one wool square right side up on your work surface. Lay the ribbon (or bias tubing) over the wool square so one end of the ribbon lines up with the edge of the square and the rest runs across the square and off the opposite side. Pin the ribbon in place.

2   Lay the other wool square, right side down, on top of the first, sandwiching the ribbon in between. Align the edges of the two squares and pin them in place. Stitch around the square with a ½" seam allowance, starting and stopping on either side of the long ribbon tail to leave an opening for turning. Backstitch at the beginning and end of your stitch line. The ribbon should hang out of the opening. Clip the corners before turning to remove bulk.

3   Turn the square right side out, then stuff it with a catnip bag. Stitch the hole closed with a slipstitch. When you need to replace the catnip, unstitch the slipstitch and refill the square.

ONE-TO-TWO-HOUR GIFTS

recycled sweater hats *Machine- and hand-sew*

Here is a very quick way to recycle an old sweater and turn it into a great new hat. With this simple pattern and a little bit of imagination, you can make a variety of styles that will work well for men, women, and children.

MATERIALS

Tracing paper, for pattern

100% wool sweater, washed and dried in a hot cycle several times to shrink

Thread to match

Hand-sewing needle

1 yard 2"-wide ribbon and thread to match (for 1920s-style cloche variation only)

Bias Blossom (see page 22) for adornment (optional)

Plastic cutting board or plastic tablecloth, for work surface

Iron and ironing board

1. Trace the hat pattern (adult or child, round or pointed top) and cut it out (see page 53).

2. Turn the sweater inside out and pin the pattern to the sweater, with the straight side along the sweater's bottom edge. Cut out two pieces together, cutting through the front and back sides of the sweater. You can also use the sleeves and upper body of the sweater to make these hats, but there is usually ribbing or another nice detail on the bottom edge that is fun to incorporate.

3. With right sides facing, pin the top of the hat, leaving the straight edge open.

4. With a ½" seam allowance, sew around the pinned edge. For the first and last 4" of this seam, backstitch ¾" for every 1" you stitch. This will give you the flexibility to trim the bottom edge, if necessary, without the seam coming apart.

5. Splay open the seam allowance and topstitch it down approximately ¼" on either side of the center seam, repeating the same backstitching technique as for the center seam. Trim off the excess seam allowance close to the topstitch. It's okay if the wool stretches as you sew or if the topstitching is not perfectly straight; the ripples in the seam line will flatten and the stitching will be less visible after you wet the hat.

6. Drench the hat with hot tap water and squeeze out the excess moisture with a towel. Turn the hat right side out. While the hat is still damp, place it on your head (or the recipient's head) with the seam running from front to back. Pull the edges down, forming the hat to your head and removing any ripples in the seam. The warm water will also fluff up the wool fibers, making any slightly uneven stitching less visible.

7 Set the iron to a wool setting and press the hat all the way around the rim. Do not stretch the wool—press in one spot only, then move to the next spot. This will speed up the drying process and tighten up the felted knit fibers.

VARIATIONS

Skullcap (uses rounded top pattern): With the damp hat on, fold the edges up above your ears to form an even brim and carefully pin in place. Remove the hat from your head and trim the folded edge to a uniform width (about 1"), if necessary. Make a running stitch along the folded edge. Before you knot off the thread, put the hat back on your head and adjust the thread tension so it is comfortable (the thread will help the hat dry to your head size). Take off the hat, knot the thread, and follow the pressing instructions given in Step 7. Let dry completely.

1920s-Style Cloche (uses rounded top pattern): With the damp hat on, pull the edges down around your head; it should come down over your ears and eyebrows. Remove the hat from your head. Measure around your head (or the recipient's head) from the forehead to the lower back of the head. Add 1" to that measurement and cut the ribbon to that length. Fold the ribbon in half with right sides facing, and stitch the ends together with a ½" seam allowance. Turn the ribbon right side out. Put the hat back on and slip the ribbon over the hat, pulling the wool edge down below the ribbon about 1" in the front and about 2" in the back (trim the edge, if necessary). Carefully pin the ribbon in place. Take off the hat and make a running stitch around the ribbon's top

and bottom edges using matching thread. Fold up the back edge of the hat over the ribbon and make a few tacking stitches to hold it in place at the seam line. Follow the pressing instructions given in Step 7. Let dry completely. Adorn with Bias Blossom, if desired.

Pointed Hat with Pompom Top (uses pointed top pattern): With the damp hat on, look in the mirror and center the seam on your forehead. With your thumbs and forefingers, grab the wool by your ears and pull down to lengthen. Fold up the center seam in the front of the hat about 1" to 1 ½" and carefully pin it in place. Do the same to the back center seam. Take off the hat and pin the brim so that it gradually narrows from the front center seam to the side point where you pulled down at the ears. Pin the back edge in the same way as the front, and gradually narrow the fold until it reaches the ear points. Stitch all folded edges down with a running stitch. Follow the pressing instructions given in Step 7. Let dry completely.

For the pompom, cut ten 5" × ¼" sweater pieces along the grain of the knit (if the sweater is ribbed, follow the rows of ribbing). Bundle all pieces together. With a needle that has been threaded and knotted, make a few stitches in the center of the bundle to secure the thread. Wrap the thread around the center of the bundle several times to bind the pieces together. Make a few more stitches to secure the wrapped thread before knotting it. Hand-stitch the pompom's bound center to the top point of the hat.

You can also make a round-top version of this hat, adding pompoms to ear ties instead of at the top. To make ear ties with pompoms, cut two 5" × ¼" sweater pieces along the grain of the knit. Whipstitch one pompom's bound center to the end of one tie. Whipstitch the other end of the tie to the inside of one earflap. Repeat for the other side. Trim the ends of the pompoms to the desired length.

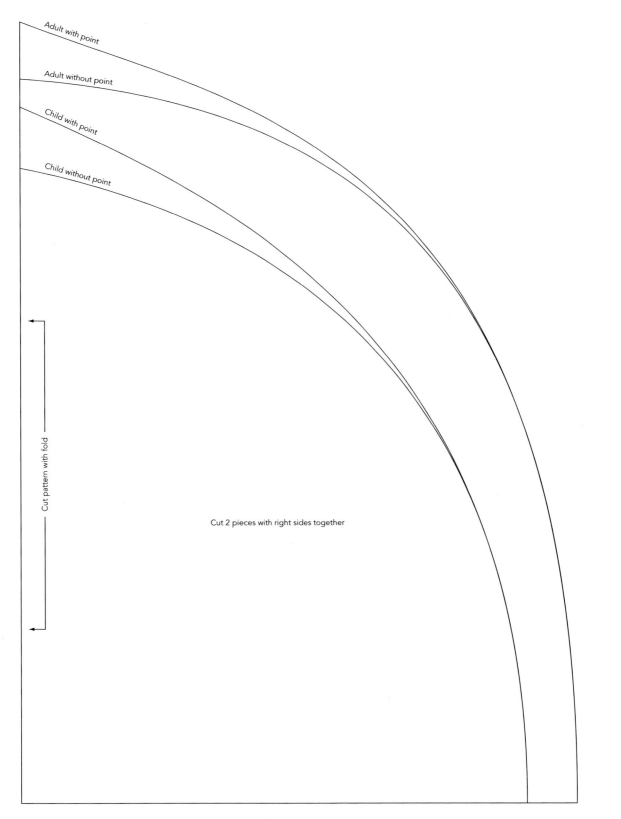

Adult with point

Adult without point

Child with point

Child without point

Cut pattern with fold

Cut 2 pieces with right sides together

Opening

cotton knit animals *Machine-sew*

I found a wonderful website (www.nearseanaturals.com) that carries only organic fabrics, and fell in love with their soft, cozy, knit fleece fabrics. I made the bear and the sheep from their organic cotton fleece, but they could be made with other knit fabrics as well, such as polar fleece or wool double knit. The stretch of the fabric affects shape: If your knit fabric is stretchier from top to bottom, the animal becomes tall (like my sheep at left); if it's stretchy from side to side, the animal becomes wide. If the knit has an even stretch in both directions, your creature will keep the shape of the pattern (like my bear). These two animals are made from exactly the same pattern; using different-colored fabric changes them into different animals. This pattern can also be used to make a pig or even a cow—with the right colors and a bit of imagination.

MATERIALS

Tracing paper, for pattern

¼ yard cotton knit fleece
(brown for bear, white for sheep)

⅛ yard cotton knit fleece in contrasting color (white for bear, black for sheep)

Thread to match both body and contrast fabric

20"–30" embroidery floss
(dark brown for bear, tan for sheep)

Several large handfuls stuffing

Hand-sewing needle

Embroidery needle

1 Trace the pattern pieces on page 57 and cut them out.

2 Pin the pattern pieces to your fabric and cut out either the bear or the sheep (or your own creation). **For the bear:** Fold the brown fabric in half so you can cut the pieces in sets of two. Cut one set of two body pieces, and one set of two outer ear pieces. Cut four leg sets (for a total of eight leg pieces). Fold the white fabric and cut one set of inner ear pieces and one snout piece. **For the sheep:** Fold the white fabric in half so you can cut the pieces in sets of two. Cut one set of two body pieces, two sets of ear pieces (for a total of four ear pieces). Fold the black fabric and cut four leg sets (for a total of eight leg pieces). For the snout, cut only one piece.

3 Pin the snout in place as marked on the pattern. Whipstitch all the way around the snout.

4 In the spot indicated on the pattern for the nose (in the center of snout), use the embroidery needle and floss to make several ¼"-long stitches on top of each other. Knot the floss on the back side of the front body piece.

5 With a ¼" seam allowance, stitch each of the four leg sets and two ear sets together, with right sides facing. Stitch only the curved edges; leave the straight edges open for turning. To stitch around these small pieces make a few stitches, stop the machine with the needle down in the work, then lift the foot to pivot the piece slightly before beginning again. Continue stitching and pivoting until you have completed the piece. Turn each leg right side out.

6 Lay the front body piece (with the snout attached) right side up on your work surface. Lay the legs on top of the body, with their open ends centered on the "leg" marks indicated on the pattern and aligned with the cut edges of the body. Orient the legs so the curve of each foot points upward toward the snout. Pin the legs in place.

7 Machine-baste the legs to the body, removing the pins as you sew.

8 Pin the back of the body to the front of the body with right sides facing and the top portion of each leg piece sandwiched in between. Stitch around the body with a ¼" seam allowance, leaving the space between the bottom legs open for turning. Turn right side out.

9 Fill the animal with stuffing and whipstitch the opening closed.

10 To create the different ear shapes for the bear and the sheep, you will need to hand-stitch the ear bases differently. **For the bear ears:** With the white side facing up, catch the fabric at the side seams of the lower right- and left-hand corners with your needle and thread, cinching the two seam lines together. Make a few stitches to hold in place. Center the cinch stitch you just made, flatten the base of the ear, and whipstitch it. (This prepares the ear to be attached to the body). Whipstitch the ears to the top of the bear's head at the "ear" marks indicated on the pattern so the white sides of the ears face the front. **For the sheep ears:** Fold the open base of the ear in half so the side seams lay one on top of the other, then whipstitch the base closed. Whipstitch the ears to the top of the sheep's head at the "ear" marks indicated on the pattern so the inner ear faces down toward the legs.

Ear Stitching

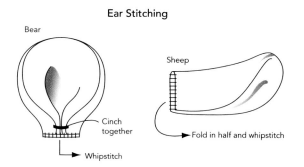

Bear

Cinch together

Whipstitch

Sheep

Fold in half and whipstitch

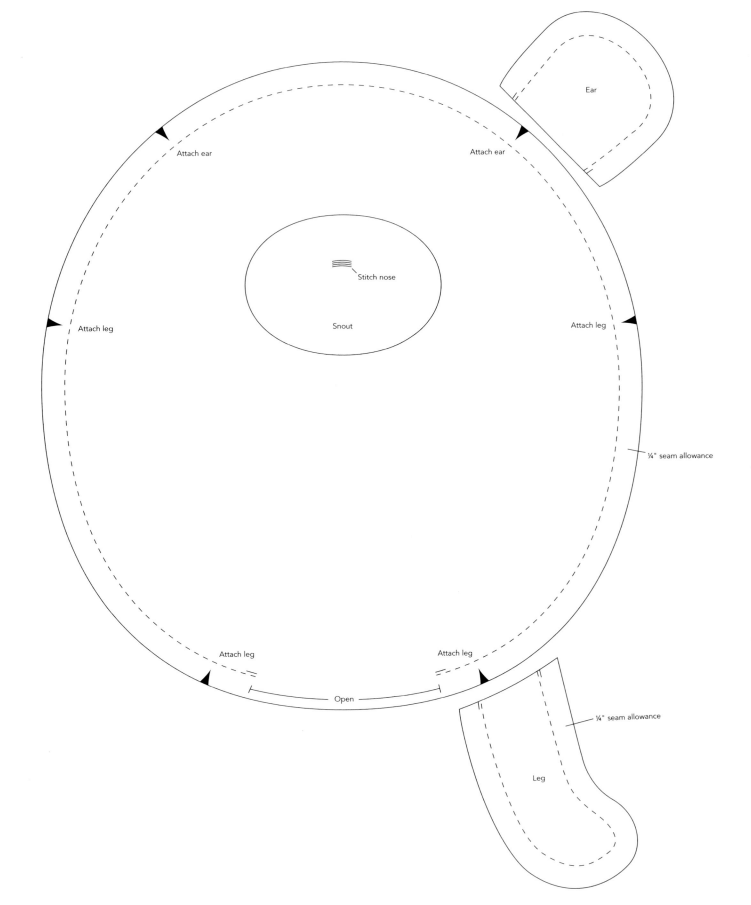

Attach ear

Ear

Attach ear

Stitch nose

Snout

Attach leg

Attach leg

¼" seam allowance

Attach leg

Attach leg

Open

¼" seam allowance

Leg

felted rocks *No-sew*

These felted rocks are such beautiful, tactile objects that I enjoy just looking at and holding them. But the truth is that I first made them expressly for their function—I use them as paperweights to keep the corners of my pattern paper from curling as I work, and to keep pattern pieces in an orderly stack. They also make a useful storage spot for stray pins.

MATERIALS

1 ounce wool roving (enough to cover 1 to 3 potato-sized rocks; see Sources on page 140)

Thread to match

1 to 3 smooth, round, or oval potato-sized rocks

Spray bottle filled with liquid soap solution (1 liter water to 1 tablespoon dish soap)

Nylon knee-high or about 8" cut from nylon stocking (including the foot)

Plastic tablecloth, to protect work surface

VARIATION

To make a wool bath scrubber, use an oval bar of soap instead of a rock.

1. Pull wisps of fibers from the end of the roving and lay them in thin, crisscrossed layers over the entire surface of the rock. If you lay all the fibers in the same direction or wrap the rock with long fibers taken from the side of the roving, the surface will not be smooth and seamless after felting. It is the crossing and layering of very fine groups of fibers that produces a smooth, seamless surface.

2. After you have layered and crossed the fibers to cover the rock with one loose layer, wrap the rock with thread, turning it as you wrap (as though you were winding a ball of yarn) to hold the fibers in place. This will keep the first layer from sliding around and slipping off the surface of the rock as you add more layers.

3. Repeat this layering and thread-wrapping process 2 to 3 more times, until the entire surface of the rock is covered.

4. Cover the rock with one final layer of wool fibers. But do not wrap this layer with thread. Carefully place the wool-covered rock into the toe of the knee-high or stocking. (You might need a second pair of hands to accomplish this without dislodging the fibers of the topmost layer.) Once the rock is in the toe, stretch the stocking and knot it so the rock is tightly encased. Try not to catch any fibers in your knot.

5. Spray the pouch with the soap solution, then begin to rub and turn it with your hands. This action, along with the lubrication of the dish soap, will help the fibers join and bond to each other. Continue vigorously rubbing and turning for 5 to 7 minutes.

6. Remove the rock from the stocking and check its progress. Repeat Step 5 until the rock is felted to your liking. If you want the felt to be thicker or if you are not pleased with the surface, repeat Steps 1–5 one more time.

fringed guest towel *Machine-sew*

There is something practical yet indulgent about linen hand towels. It's a secret pleasure of mine to make up a guest room for a visiting friend with flowers and beautiful fresh linens. When I use a crisp linen hand towel, I feel pampered and am reminded of those wonderful old paintings that depict linen cabinets full of perfectly folded sheets and towels. The little touch of red and the fringe on the ends of this towel were inspired by a photo in a book about the history of linens that I love and often refer to.

MATERIALS

17" × 32" piece linen (cut on grain of fabric, see page 130)

Two ⅜" × 17" pieces bias trim

Thread to match

Hand-sewing needle (optional)

Iron and ironing board

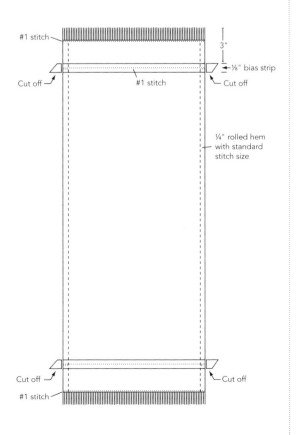

1   To fringe the 17" ends of the linen, make a stitch line 1" in from either end using a very small stitch length (#1 on most machines). This will secure the fabric from fraying beyond the stitched line. Then fringe the ends of the towel by removing the horizontal fibers from the vertical fibers up to the stitched line. You may want to use a pin to ease them out. Repeat on the other 17" side.

2   Make a rolled hem on the long sides by pressing each edge over about ¼" with your iron, then roll each edge over another ¼" and press again. Don't worry about the exact measurement of this rolled hem—visual consistency is more important, and I find it more enjoyable and less time consuming to fold the edge by eye rather than by meticulous measuring. Topstitch the rolled hems down with the sewing machine or by hand using a fell stitch.

3   Pin each bias strip to right side of towel, about 3" from each of the short ends. Stitch down the center of the length of bias strip, backstitching at each rolled edge of the linen. The bias may stretch slightly when you stitch it on; if it does, just trim off the ends that extend beyond the linen's edge after you complete this stitch. There is no need to finish the ends of the bias in any way.

4   To fringe the bias strips, spray them with water, then rough up the edges with your fingers to separate the fibers. You can fold the bias strips in half to cover the stitching or just leave it a bit ruffled.

patchwork pillow *Machine-sew*

Patchwork pillows are a good way to use small pieces of fabric leftover from past projects. The body of this pillow is linen; the patched strip in this pillow is a mix of wool, linen, and cotton. I like to use fabrics of a light to medium weight so the seams press flat. If you want to add a simple zipper to this pillow, refer to page 135 before cutting the back.

MATERIALS

Eight 8" × 3" scraps fabric, in coordinating colors, for patchwork panel (see Note)

One 4" × 18" and one 9" × 18" piece linen, for front

18" × 18" piece linen, for back

Thread to match linen

22" polyester all-purpose zipper (optional, see above)

18" pillow insert

Iron and ironing board

Rotary cutter and cutting mat

Clear plastic ruler

1   On a sewing machine set at a very small stitch length (#1 on most machines) and using a ¼" seam allowance, stitch the fabric scraps together, right sides facing, along their 8" edges to create a single strip that measures 8" wide by approximately 20" long. (The strip must be at least 18" long when stitched together.)

2   Press the seams open on the back of the panel.

3   Lay the panel on the rotary cutting mat. Using the rotary cutter and ruler, trim the strip so it measures 7" × 18".

4   With a ½" seam allowance, stitch the 4" × 18" and 9" × 18" linen pieces to the 18" sides of the patchwork strip so the patchwork is flanked by the two linen pieces. You should have an 18" × 18" square; this is the front of the pillow. Press the seams open on the back.

5   With right sides facing, pin the front and back of the pillow together. Sew around all four sides, leaving a 14" opening along the bottom edge. Turn the pillow cover right side out and press it. Stuff with the pillow insert, and stitch the 14" opening closed with a slipstitch.

Note: If you want a more random patched look, you can use 8" × 4" scraps and angle some of them. Just be sure the resulting strip is at least 18" long when stitched together.

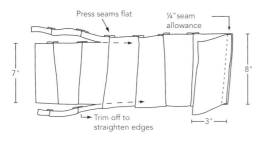

Press seams flat   ¼" seam allowance   7"   8"   Trim off to straighten edges   3"

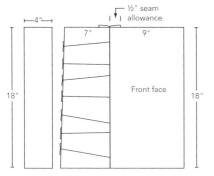

½" seam allowance   4"   7"   9"   18"   Front face   18"

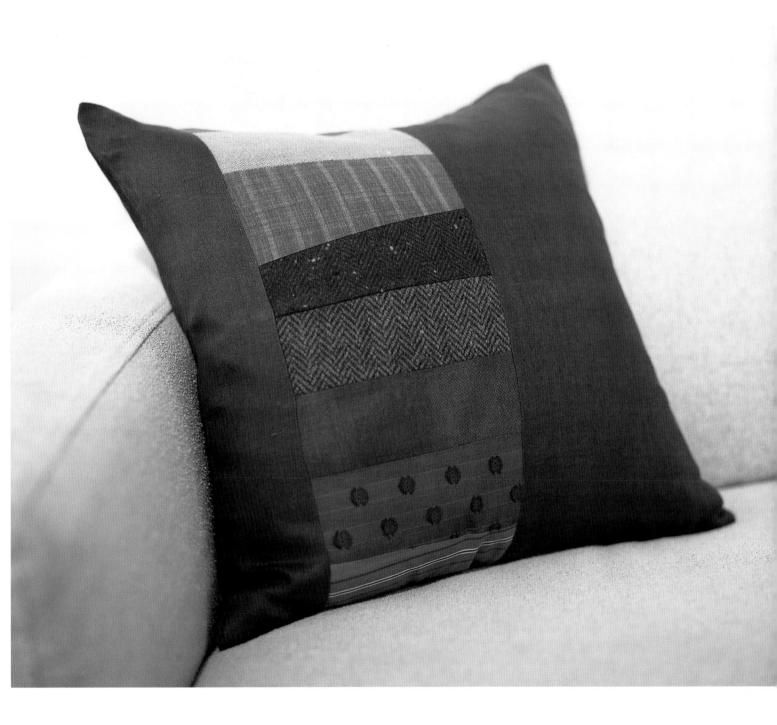

red cross appliquéd pillow

Machine- and hand-sew

This graphic pillow is a soft, cozy gift for a friend in need of some TLC. The directions below are for making a red cross and applying it to an 18" pillow, but the emblematic cross can be adapted for many other gifts, such as a hot water bottle cover, a premade pillowcase, or a special blanket. If you are making a pillow and want to add a simple zipper, refer to page 135 before cutting the back.

MATERIALS

13" × 13" piece red linen

Two 18" × 18" pieces linen, in contrasting color

Thread to match

Hand-sewing needle

22" polyester all-purpose zipper (optional; see headnote)

18" pillow insert

Fray Check

Iron and ironing board

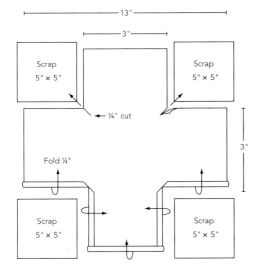

1 Cut a 5" × 5" square from each corner of the red linen, making a cross shape.

2 To fold under all the edges of the cross appliqué, make a ¼" cut at a 45-degree angle in each of the four interior corners of the cross. Dab a small amount of Fray Check on each ¼" corner cut to secure the fibers. Use the Fray Check sparingly—it can flow out faster than you expect.

3 Press all the edges ¼" in toward the center of the cross (eight interior side edges and four end edges). Flip the cross over and pin it right side up and centered on one of the 18" × 18" linen pieces.

4 Baste the edges of the cross to hold it in place. Using a fell stitch, appliqué the cross to the pillow front.

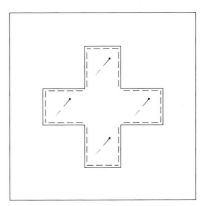

5 With right sides facing, pin the front and back of the pillow together. Sew around all four sides, leaving a 14" opening along the bottom edge. Turn the pillow cover right side out and press it. Stuff with the pillow insert and stitch the 14" opening closed with a slipstitch.

travel pouch *Machine-sew*

This little pouch is handy for so many things. Use it to hold toiletries, makeup, or jewelry. It even makes a great little bag to carry supplies in when sewing on the go. You will be stitching through several layers of fabric, so choose a lightweight but durable fabric that your machine can handle.

MATERIALS

11½" × 13" piece fabric, for outside

11½" × 13" piece fabric, for lining

Two 2" × ½" pieces twill tape, folded in half and stitched at cut ends to form loops

Two 3½" × 1¾" pieces lining fabric, for interior binding

Thread to match outside fabric

18" polyester all-purpose zipper to match

Fabri-Tac adhesive

Hand-sewing needle (optional)

Iron and ironing board

1   Lay the two 11½" × 13" fabric pieces with right sides together. Pin the 11½" sides together and stitch with a ¼" seam allowance. Turn the fabric right side out and press the seams so they lay flat.

2   Topstitch the two open sides with a ¼" seam allowance to keep them from shifting.

3   Lay the fabric, lining side up, on your work surface with the finished, pressed edges running vertically. Lay the zipper, closed and face up, on the lining so it is parallel to the finished edges. Let the zipper ends hang over the cut fabric edges. (Because of the zipper's extra length, the zipper pull should be out of your way the entire time you are sewing.) Fold the finished edges in, one at a time, so they rest along either side of the zipper teeth. Baste them in place. Unzip the zipper, then machine-stitch the basted edges down to the zipper tape; you can also hand-sew them using a fell stitch.

4   Turn the work so the lining is on the outside. Zip the zipper until the pull is about 1" from the open edge. Trim the zipper ends flush with the open edge. At both ends of the zipper, make a tacking stitch that wraps around the teeth. This will keep the pull from coming off either end. Adjust the pouch so the zipper runs through its center, with 3" of fabric on either side of it.

Step 3 (through basting)

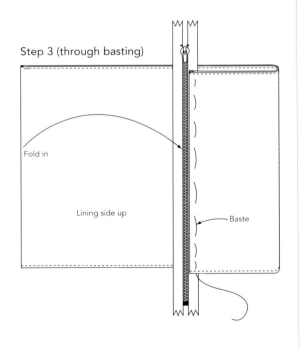

Fold in

Lining side up

Baste

5   Insert the folded end of a twill tape loop between the fabric layers at each end of the zipper. Match the cut ends of the loops with the open edges of the fabric, center so the zipper teeth run down the middle of each loop, and pin in place.

6   Pin the open fabric edge 1" to the left and 1" to the right of the zipper's center line on both ends of the tube. With a ¼" seam allowance, stitch this middle section (from pin to pin and over the zipper) on both ends of the tube.

7   Press in one of the unstitched corners toward the end of your last stitch, then fold the flaps created by this action so they wrap around the front and back of the work. Pin the flaps in place. Repeat for remaining corners. With a ¼" seam allowance, stitch both ends of the tube to hold the pinned flaps in place.

8   Center the 3½" edge of one of the binding pieces, right side up, under the end of the tube, matching the edges. With a ¼" seam allowance, stitch across the end of the tube to attach the binding fabric. Repeat for the other end.

9   Flip this piece of fabric up so it hangs off the end of the tube. Fold the side flaps and glue them in place with Fabri-Tac adhesive. Fold the end up so its edge butts up to the end of the pouch, glue in place, then fold the end up once more and glue it in place to completely encase the raw end of the seam allowance. Repeat for other end. Turn pouch right side out.

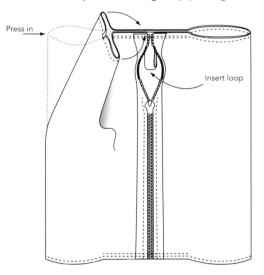

Steps 5–7 (through flap pinning)

Insert loop

Press in

Step 7 (stitching pinned flaps)

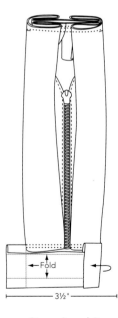

Fold

3½"

Steps 8 and 9
(stitch binding, fold and glue)

TWO-TO-THREE-HOUR GIFTS

silk-trimmed wool blanket
*Machine-
and hand-sew*

This double-faced wool blanket is a luxurious way to stay warm on a chilly day. Its ends are trimmed in silk using a simple but elegant folded bias technique, and the selvage edges are left unadorned, becoming the blanket's sides. The finished blanket is 90" long and 54" wide, which is a suitable size for a twin bed or to use as a throw on a large couch.

MATERIALS

Two strips 3"-wide silk bias, each at least 56" long (connected if necessary; see page 132)

2½ yards double-faced wool, 54" wide

Thread to match silk

Iron and ironing board

Rotary cutter and rotary cutting mat

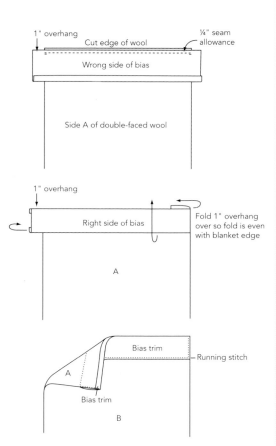

1" overhang
¼" seam allowance
Cut edge of wool
Wrong side of bias
Side A of double-faced wool

1" overhang
Right side of bias
Fold 1" overhang over so fold is even with blanket edge
A

Bias trim
Running stitch
A
Bias trim
B

1 Press a ¼" fold along the length of one side of each bias strip.

2 Lay one bias strip, fold side up, on top of each 54" weft (cut) end of the wool, leaving a 1" overhang on either side of the wool. The cut edges of bias and wool should align. With a ¼" seam allowance, stitch the long side of the bias strip to the cut edge of the wool.

3 Fold the bias strip back over the seam line and the cut edge of the wool to the opposite side of the blanket. This creates a narrow silk trim on one side of the wool and a wide trim on the other.

4 Fold the 1" bias overhangs on the left and right sides of the blanket in toward the center of the blanket. Press flat.

5 Pin the ¼" pressed bias edge (from Step 1) in place and hand-stitch the folded edges of the silk trim to the wool with a small running stitch. You can also stitch the silk edge by machine with a zigzag stitch, making the process faster.

6 Repeat Steps 1–5 on the opposite end of the blanket.

hand-stitched scarf *Hand-sew*

This elegant scarf requires no machine-stitching and can be made in a variety of fabrics, such as lightweight wool, silk gauze, or two tones of tissue-weight linen—as long as the edges fringe nicely. You could even use a combination of two fabrics, like silk and wool. When choosing fabric at a store, ask for a swatch to test the fringing, or ask if you can test the edge before it's cut to make sure the fibers are not too difficult to separate. To make my running stitch design, I used silk thread, which has a wonderful luster and slides smoothly through the fabric, but embroidery thread or machine thread are fine alternatives. Hand-stitching has such a special quality and is so unusual to see that this gift will truly be a beautiful surprise.

MATERIALS

⅜ yard lightweight fabric, 45"–54" wide, for front

⅜ yard lightweight fabric, 45"–54" wide, for back

Thread in contrasting color

Hand-sewing needle

Water-erasable marking pen (optional)

Spray bottle filled with water (optional)

Iron and ironing board

Note: Depending on the fabric you choose the fringe may be delicate, so wash this scarf gently by hand in cold water and line- dry, or dry-clean, if you prefer.

1. Cut both fabric pieces on the grain (see page 130) to 10" wide by the original width of your fabric (45" to 54"). This will prepare the fabric for fringing.

2. Fringe the short ends first by pulling out the threads that run parallel to the fabric's selvage. The depth of the fringe will increase as you remove threads. Continue to remove threads until the fringe is ¼" deep. Fringe both ends and both sides of the front and back pieces.

3. Lay the two pieces on top of each other on your work surface with long edges aligning. One piece may be a bit longer than the other—this is fine. Place the shorter piece on top, and center it lengthwise on the longer piece.

4. Make a large basting stitch around the edges of the scarf inside the fringing line. This will hold the two pieces together while you make your decorative running stitch, and will be taken out when you are finished.

5. Use a small running stitch (about ⅛") to create a simple pattern that holds the two pieces together. The pattern does not have to cover the entire scarf; it can be at both ends and not in the center or even scattered randomly—just make sure it covers enough of the surface to keep the two pieces from shifting too much. You can draw the pattern with a water-erasable pen or just stitch it freehand. When you are finished, remove the large basting stitches, spray the scarf with water if needed to remove the pen marks, and press the scarf.

reversible hooded
towel/blanket *Machine-sew*

I thought that a twist on the hooded towel was in order, so I decided to make a version that is a linen towel on one side and a flannel blanket on the other. It turned out to be a cozy hooded blanket, an absorbent towel, and the perfect wrap for drying off after a run through the sprinkler. To make it fit children of different sizes, simply increase or decrease the size of the square pieces. This towel is shown on Alex, size 3T, and Sam, boys' size 5–6.

MATERIALS

1 yard 54"-wide linen, prewashed

1 yard 54"-wide cotton flannel, prewashed (if fabric is narrower than 54", you'll need an additional ½ yard fabric for both linen and cotton sides)

Thread to match linen and flannel

Iron and ironing board

1   Cut out two 34" × 34" squares, one linen and one cotton flannel, for the body of the towel.

2   For the hood, cut out two right triangles, one linen and one cotton flannel, that have two equal 14½" sides.

3   Place the linen and cotton triangles together with right sides facing. Stitch the long sides of the triangles together with a ½" seam allowance. Turn the triangle right side out and press the seam.

4   Topstitch the edge of the seam, guiding the edge of your machine foot along the edge of the fabric to achieve an even stitch. (The width is not critical, and will vary depending on the actual size of your machine's straight stitching foot.) It is important to secure the interior seam allowance so it will not unravel after multiple washings.

5   Lay the flannel square, right side up, on your work surface. Place the triangle, flannel side down, on top of the flannel square so the right angle of the triangle matches up with one of the corners of the square. Lay the linen square right side down on top of the flannel square, sandwiching the triangle between them. Pin all four sides of the square together.

6   Stitch around all four sides of the square with a ½" seam allowance, leaving a 4" hole (more if you are using thick fabric) on one side of the square to turn the towel. Backstitch at the beginning and end of your stitch line.

7   Turn the towel right side out and stitch the hole closed with a slip stitch. Press the edges flat.

8 Topstitch around the edge of the blanket. Begin and end your
   stitch line on either side of the hood's topstitch, connecting the
   topstitches so there appears to be one continuous stitch
   all the way around the hood and blanket edges. The hood's
   sides (up to the point) should be the only area without
   topstitching. Alternatively, rather than topstitching to secure
   the interior edge, you can also zigzag stitch around the seam
   allowances on the inside before turning the towel right side out.

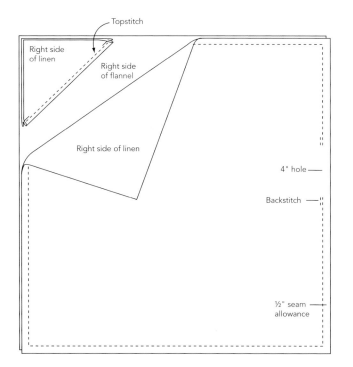

Topstitch

Right side
of linen

Right side
of flannel

Right side of linen

4" hole

Backstitch

½" seam
allowance

felted silk scarf *Nearly no-sew*

I had wanted to experiment with this felting process for a long time, having seen items made using variations of it in small boutiques. The delicate tonal layer of wool felted over chiffon shrinks to create a beautifully textured, lightweight yet incredibly warm scarf. The printed version here was made with a very lightweight silk scarf I found in an antiques store. I love the way the thin layer of felt softens and slightly obscures the print. The other samples are made with chiffon strips torn from the weft of the bolt. The wool fibers felt over the edges of the torn fabric, so there is no finishing required on the edges.

MATERIALS

Two 10"-wide strips silk chiffon (solid or print), 45" or longer, with torn edges

Thread to match silk chiffon

Two pieces cotton voile or nylon netting, several inches wider and longer than final scarf length (about 80" to 90")

1–2 ounces merino wool roving, color-coordinated with fabric (see Sources on page 140)

Water-safe work surface covered with a canvas drop cloth (secure drop cloth to table so it won't move)

Spray bottle filled with liquid soap solution (1 liter water to 1 tablespoon dish soap)

Clothes dryer

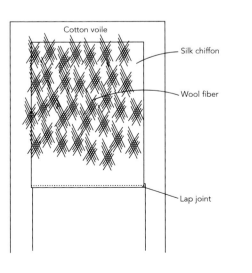

1. To connect the two pices of chiffon, overlap the short end of one to the short end of the other by ¼" and make a running stitch across the lapped seam. Cut the length down to about 70", and set the extra chiffon aside for another project.

2. Lay one piece cotton voile or nylon netting on your water-safe work surface and center the silk strip over it. Pull wisps of fibers from the end of the roving and lay them in a thin, crisscrossed layer over the silk strip, letting the fibers slightly overhang the edges of the silk. When the silk strip is completely covered, spray it with the soap solution, evenly covering the fibers. (Spraying from directly above the scarf helps keep the fibers in place.)

3. Gently lay the second piece of voile or netting on top of the wet fiber layer, being careful not to dislodge any of the wool. Flip the layers over (you may want a friend to help). Carefully lift the voile or netting to expose the other side of the silk not yet covered by the wool fibers. Layer the fibers as in Step 2. When the silk strip is completely covered, spray it with the soap solution, as in Step 2, and gently replace the voile or netting layer.

4. Roll the layered bundle lengthwise. Cover the bundle with your hands and press firmly into the work surface, rolling it away from you as if kneading bread. Rotate the bundle a half turn and press and roll again. Repeat this motion 30 to 40 times. Unroll the bundle, then reroll it from the opposite side. Repeat the kneading action.

5 Unroll the bundle, fold the length in thirds, and roll the longer side. Knead the bundle again, as in Step 4 (this time you are kneading across the width of the scarf). Unroll the bundle, reroll it from the opposite side, and knead for the last time. Unroll and unfold the bundle, carefully lifting the voile to check the felting process. The fibers should be holding together and forming a skin over the silk, but should not yet be fully felted. (If the fibers don't appear to be holding together, repeat Steps 4–5.)

6 When a skin has begun to form over the silk, gently remove both voile pieces, being careful not to pull the wool fibers away from the silk. Wet the scarf in a bowl of warm water. Remove the scarf from the bowl and squeeze out any excess water. Carefully open the scarf and place it in a dryer set to tumble dry on high heat. Place a T-shirt or a small towel in the dryer to help agitate the scarf. This final felting process is called *fulling*.

Note: Hand-wash and line-dry.

VARIATION

Try embellishing the scarf with small silk Bias Blossoms (page 22). Use 2"-wide bias strips to make the same size blossoms you see in the photograph on page 80.

silk sarong *Hand-sew*

It is hard not to love rectangular garments—sarongs, shawls, and saris are elegant and elemental items of clothing, a celebration of fabric in its pure and uncut form. The only change I have made to the traditional sarong is to add ties that reduce the fabric bulk at the waist and make it more comfortable to wear. I like to hand-stitch the rolled hem because I think this is a beautiful, subtle detail, but you can also use a machine to shorten the time it takes to make this project.

MATERIALS

2 yards lightweight silk (cotton or linen also work well)

Thread to match

2 yards ribbon, ½"–¾" wide, for ties

Iron and ironing board

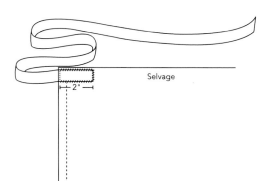

Selvage

2"

1 Cut the fabric to 64" long for a size 4/6 or 68" for a size 8/10. (For each additional size range, add about 4".)

2 The width of the fabric will become the length of the sarong (hip to floor). If the wearer is tall, you may not need to hem either of the selvage edges. If the sarong needs shortening, cut one of the selvage edges off so the fabric is ½" longer than the desired length of the sarong.

3 Finish the bottom and sides with a ¼" rolled hem. To make a rolled hem on the bottom edge, fold and press the edge over ¼", then fold and press it over ¼" again. Pin the ¼" hem in place. Repeat on the remaining two sides. Stitch the edge of the rolled hem on all three pinned sides using a running stitch or machine-stitch the rolled hems.

4 To make the ties, cut the ribbon into two 1-yard pieces. Fold one end of the ribbon ¼". Pin the folded end 2" in on the upper right-hand corner of the outside of the silk, parallel to the selvage edge. Use a whipstitch to attach the ribbon to the sarong corner, stitching all the way around three sides of the ribbon as shown in the illustration. Then insert your needle through to the back of the fabric and stitch the corner of the sarong to the back of the ribbon. Knot your thread in the back when this is complete. Repeat with the second ribbon piece on the left-hand corner of the sarong.

tweed scarf *Machine- and hand-sew*

This tweed scarf, in a soft merino or plush cashmere, will be a warm and welcome autumn gift. You will only need about ⅓ yard fabric (44" or wider), as the width of the fabric becomes the length of the scarf. For the fringe, I found that yarns with a good twist seem to work the best. Also, the plusher the yarn, the fewer strands you'll need to create a fluffy fringe. The Misti Alpaca Chunky (shown in cream on page 89) is a dream to work with—fluffy and extremely soft. The merino and silk blend from Alchemy (shown in green at left and in blue on page 89) has a beautiful sheen and softness, but is denser and thinner than the Misti Alpaca, so it requires twice as many strands to get the same fullness.

MATERIALS

Wool tweed, 44" or wider, cut to 11" (if using Misti Alpaca Chunky for fringe), or to 9" (if using Alchemy Synchronicity for fringe)

About 25 yards Misti Alpaca Chunky (100% alpaca) or about 50 yards Alchemy Synchronicity (50% silk; 50% merino wool)

Thread to match tweed

Tapestry needle, size 13

Rotary cutter and cutting mat

Clear plastic ruler

Step 4

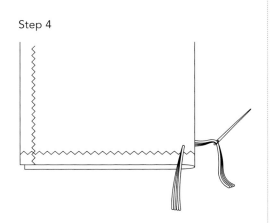

1 Make a ½" fold along all four sides of the tweed, and pin in place. Zigzag stitch the folds, catching the cut edges in the center of the zigzag. The closer the thread matches the tweed, the less visible this stitch will be. Backstitch as you complete the last side.

2 For each fringed tassel, fold the yarn as follows: For Misti Alpaca Chunky, cut a 45" length and fold it in half twice so you have four strands of yarn. For Alchemy Synchronicity, cut two 45" lengths and put them side by side with their ends lined up. Fold them in half twice so you have eight strands of yarn.

3 Thread the folded ends of the yarn bundle through the eye of the tapestry needle. The large eye should easily accommodate the folded yarn.

4 Fold one of the short ends of the scarf in half, wrong sides together, to find its center. Insert the needle through the center fold, just above your zigzag stitch. The blunt end of the tapestry needle should separate the tweed fibers and pass through the fabric easily. Pull the yarn strands through the fabric until there is an equal amount of yarn on each side. (When you make a stitch through the fold of your fabric, your yarn will pass from front to back to front again in one stitch, creating a loop on the opposite side of the fabric that you can pull the tails of the yarn through to make the fringe.)

5 Thread the yarn ends from the front of the scarf through the loop in the back and pull them taut to make a fringe.

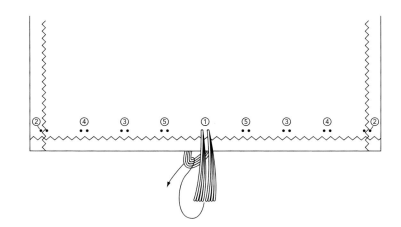

6 The next two fringe sections you make will be on either corner of the scarf. Insert your needle just above the zigzag on the scarf end and centered on the zigzag side seam. Repeat Steps 2–5 to make the corner fringe sections.

7 For the remaining fringe sections (nine total across each end), bisect the right and left sides between the end and center fringe sections, and add fringe to those two points. Then bisect the remaining four sections, adding fringe to each of those points.

8 Repeat on the other end of the scarf in the same manner, following Steps 2–7.

9 When the fringe is complete, lay the scarf on your cutting mat. Trim the ends with the rotary cutter and ruler to achieve an even fringe about 3" long.

twig-handle tote   *Machine- and hand-sew*

This bag is just the right size for throwing in a few things on your way out the door—the book you're reading or a sewing or knitting project. Fill it with flowers and treats for someone special and it becomes a thoughtful gift. Natural linen, twig handles, and a beautiful shell button give it a distinctly organic feel.

MATERIALS

15" × 24" piece linen, for outside

15" × 24" piece linen in contrast color, for lining

Four 3" × 10" pieces linen, for handle straps

1¼" × 10" strip linen bias, stitched and turned, for button loop (see page 133)

Thread to match

Hand-sewing needle

1 shell button, 1½" in diameter

Two 9" × ½" twigs, ends slightly sanded (for bamboo handles of the same size, see Sources on page 140)

Button thread, top stitching thread, or another sturdy thread to match bag fabric

Iron and ironing board

Tube turner

Fabri-Tac adhesive

1. Fold the 15" × 24" piece outside fabric in half, with right sides facing, so it measures 15" × 12". The cut edges will become the top opening of the bag and the folded edge will become the center bottom.

2. Along the top edge of the bag (doubled from folding) mark a point 4½" in from either corner. Make a ¼" cut through both layers of the fabric at these two points. This will mark the placement of the handle straps. Bisect the top edge and mark the center point with a ¼" cut into the fabric edge, this time cutting through only one layer. This will mark the button loop placement.

3. Cut a 2" × 2½" rectangle from the bottom right- and left-hand corners of the bag. The 2½" measurement should run along the bottom fold, and the 2" measurement up the side.

4. Pin the sides of the bag with a ½" seam allowance and stitch them together, backstitching at the beginning and end of seam. Press the seams open.

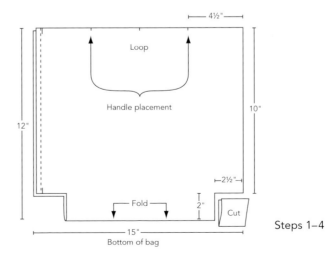

Steps 1–4

5   To form the square base of the bag, join the right bottom center fold line to the right side seam, creating an upside down T shape. Pin the bottom corner seam and stitch across it with a ½" seam allowance, backstitching at the beginning and end of seam. Repeat on the left side.

Step 5

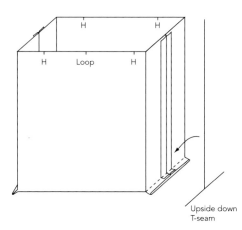

Upside down
T-seam

6   Repeat Steps 3–5 with the lining fabric, leaving a 4" hole in one side seam for turning.

7   To make the handle straps, fold each small linen piece in half lengthwise. With a ½" seam allowance, stitch the long sides of each piece together. Using the tube turner, turn the handle straps right side out and press them flat. Fold each strap in half, pinning the cut ends to form a looped strap.

8   To make the button loop, fold the linen bias strip in half and whipstitch the tube ends together, starting at the cut ends and continuing until you have stitched 2½" (you may need to adjust the amount of stitching depending on your button size). Knot off and cut the thread.

9   Center the cut ends of the looped handle straps over each of the ¼" cuts you made in Step 2 and pin them in place. Center and pin the cut end of the button loop to the cut you made in Step 3. To assemble the bag, turn the outside linen piece so the seam allowances are on the outside, and the lining linen so its seam allowances are on the inside. Slide the lining into the outside bag so their right sides are facing and their seam allowances are exposed, and pin the circumference of the opening. Stitch around the circumference with a ½" seam allowance, catching the handles and button loop as you stitch. Backstitch as you complete the circle.

10   Turn the bag right side out through the 4" opening that you left in the side of the lining. Stitch the hole closed with a whipstitch, tuck the lining into the bag, and press the top edge of the bag flat.

11   Topstitch the circumference of the opening, guiding the edge of your machine foot along the edge of the fabric to achieve an even stitch. (The width is not critical, and will vary depending on the actual size of your machine's straight stitching foot.)

12 To attach the handles, slip each twig inside two of the looped linen straps. Adjust the straps so they fall about ½" from the ends of the twigs. Glue the twigs to the insides of the linen straps with Fabri-Tac adhesive. Pinch the loop tightly just below the twig, and, using sturdy thread and the hand-sewing needle, make a running stitch just below the twig through both sides of the fabric. Securely knot off your thread and repeat for the remaining strap.

Step 12

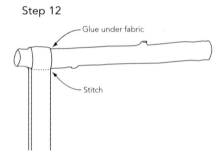

Glue under fabric

Stitch

13 Mark the button placement with a pin using the button loop as a guide. Sew on the button using the same strong thread used for the handle. Knot off thread behind button on inside of bag to hide.

MORE-THAN-THREE-HOUR GIFTS

baby quilt   *Machine- and hand-sew*

With a simple pattern of large blocks of color, this quilt can be finished in a few hours. Fill it with warm wool batting and it will be a favorite keepsake.

MATERIALS

Two 32" × 32" pieces cotton gauze

32" × 32" piece wool batting

4 pieces shirting- or quilting-weight cotton: 31" × 11" piece, for front top; 31" × 6" piece, for front middle; 31" × 16" piece, for front bottom; 31" × 31" piece, for back

Five ¾" pieces colorful wool felt

3" doll needle

Large embroidery needle

Embroidery floss

Iron and ironing board

1   Make the quilt interior: Place the two pieces of gauze on top of each other and pin the sides. With a ½" seam allowance, stitch around three sides, leaving the fourth side open. Turn the gauze piece inside out and place the wool batting inside the gauze pocket. Machine-stitch the open side closed with the seam allowance on the outside (don't worry about this unfinished seam; it will be hidden inside the quilt). With the doll needle, sew basting stitches in a grid across the entire gauze-covered wool batting, piercing through all three layers with each stitch. Start basting 2" in from the edge and make your rows 2" apart. This will keep the wool from shifting and separating.

2   Sew the blanket front: With a ½" seam allowance and right sides together, stitch the 11"-wide cotton piece to the 6"-wide cotton piece along the 31" sides. Then add the 16"-wide piece to the 6"-wide piece in the same way. Press the seams open.

3   Sew the front to the back: Pin the front of the quilt to the back piece, right sides together. With a ½" seam allowance, stitch around all four sides, leaving a 15" opening on the fourth side and backstitching at the beginning and end of your seams. Turn the quilt right side out and press the sides flat. Stuff the quilt with the gauze-covered wool batting. Using a slipstitch, hand-sew the 15" opening closed.

4   Tack the corners: Using an embroidery needle and floss, make a tacking stitch just inside the four corners of the blanket. Make sure you pierce through all the quilt layers in order to secure the interior batting to the corners of the cover.

5   Stitch on the felt squares: On the front of the quilt, pin the five wool felt squares down the center of the middle panel, approximately 5" apart. Use a tacking stitch to sew the squares down to the quilt, piercing through all the quilt layers. This will further secure the batting in the center of the quilt.

wool knit shibori scarf *No-sew*

Shibori is a traditional Japanese technique of binding, tying, clamping, or twisting—then dyeing—textiles to give them three-dimensional surfaces. In this simple example, buttons are bound into wool knit and then the fabric is shrunk around them. I used Rit dye for a two-tone color effect, but if you are looking for a project with no mess at all, try this with a wool knit in your favorite color and skip the dyeing process entirely. Be sure to use pure wool to ensure shrinkage. One yard wool knit (54" wide before shrinking) makes two scarves, each approximately 46" long after the process is completed. (The length of the scarf comes from the width of the fabric.)

MATERIALS

1 yard 100% single-knit wool jersey (soft merino is a good choice)

24 plastic buttons, ¾" in diameter (any size will work, try mixing the sizes for an irregular look)

1 spool nylon-bonded thread or another sturdy thread, for tying

Washing machine and dryer

Rubber gloves

Plastic tablecloth or garbage bag, for work surface

Small glass or plastic bowl, to fit 1 cup liquid

1 8-ounce bottle Rit liquid dye

Large glass or plastic bowl, to soak scarf

Plastic wrap

1 small paintbrush

Trimming scissors

Notes: The shrinkage of wool knits varies, but you should estimate losing approximately one-third of the length in shrinkage, as well as a lesser portion of the width. Calculate your yardage accordingly, and have extra fabric on hand if possible.

The scarf must be dry-cleaned in order to maintain its shape.

1. Wash and dry the wool jersey on high heat three times, or until you are satisfied with the shrinkage. The ends of the wool do not need any stitching, as the shrinking and felting secure the fibers, bonding them together naturally.

2. Cut two 10"-wide strips from the width of the fabric. Each strip will make one scarf.

3. One at a time, place the buttons, about 2" apart, in a line down the center length of the wool. Stretch the wool tightly up over and around each button. Wrap thread around the gathered wool of each button several times and secure it with a double knot. Continue adding buttons until you have a line down the center of the scarf (about 24 buttons). Alternatively, arrange the buttons in your own pattern.

4. Machine-wash your scarf in hot water with the buttons tied in place. If you do not plan to dye the scarf, machine-dry it on hot until it is completely dry, then untie and remove the buttons. If you plan to dye your scarf, set the scarf aside and prepare your dyes (the scarf must be damp when you dye it so the dye is absorbed evenly.)

5 Cut a strip of plastic wrap as long as the scarf. Pierce little holes along its length at the points where the buttons are tied in. Lay the damp scarf down on your work surface, buttons facing up, and place the sheet of plastic wrap over the scarf. Pop the buttons through the holes in the plastic wrap—this will protect the body of the fabric during the dyeing process.

6 Organize your dyeing materials. You may want to wear rubber gloves and cover your work surface with a plastic tablecloth or garbage bag to protect your hands and your table. Pour a cup of boiling water into the small bowl and mix in a heavy concentration (3 to 4 tablespoons) of Rit dye. Fill the larger bowl three-quarters full with very hot tap water and mix in 1 to 2 tablespoons dye. (The cooler water and smaller amount of dye creates a lighter shade.)

7 Using a small paintbrush, apply the more concentrated dye in the smaller bowl to the button heads. If you want the button heads to be darker, add more dye until you reach the desired shade.

8 With the plastic wrap still in place, rinse out the excess dye on the button heads. You can do this outdoors by laying the scarf on a plastic tablecloth or garbage bag and spraying it with cold water from a hose, or by laying it in your bathtub and rinsing it with a showerhead. Remove the plastic wrap.

9 To dye the body of the scarf, place the scarf in the larger dye bowl, agitate gently, and immediately remove from the bowl. If you want a darker color, repeat, or increase the dye concentration by adding more dye to the water. Although not necessary, dyeing the body of the scarf will help blend any dye that may have seeped into it from the buttons.

10 Rinse the scarf under cold water and machine-dry. When the scarf is completely dry, untie the thread and remove the buttons. The fabric will hold the shape of the buttons.

Dyeing the buttons

After buttons have been removed

garden play mat *Machine-sew*

This soft sculpture garden is the perfect gift for children who love their vegetables—or maybe just their felt rabbits (page 36). The mat has a hole for the rabbit to tuck into, rows of sprouting green linen vegetables to hop through, and a moveable white picket-fence. Ideally, the fabric in this project should have cut edges that you don't have to hem. I used a combination of wool felt for the grass and felted wool knit bouclé for the brown earth; you could also substitute Ultrasuede or even polar fleece for the felt.

MATERIALS

15" × 18" piece dark green wool felt

9" × 11" piece brown wool felt

15¾" × 18¾" piece light green wool felt

6" × 6" piece green linen

40" piece buckram, at least 2½" wide, cut into one 2" × 20" strip and two ¼" × 40" strips (see Note)

Thread to match felt and buckram

Water-erasable marking pen

Trimming scissors

Circle template with 1" hole

Rotary cutter and cutting mat

Clear plastic ruler

½" wide adhesive tape

Note: Buckram is a very stiff fabric that is used to stabilize the tops of curtains, among other things. It is available at most fabric stores and is sold by the yard from a roll. It comes in various widths and can be cut down if you are not able to find 2½". It is heavily sized and its edges won't fray, so it works well for the fence. If it becomes wrinkled or misshapen with use, ironing it will bring it back to shape again.

1 Lay the dark green felt flat on your work surface. Center the brown felt on top of it and pin it in place. Stitch the brown piece to the green piece around the sides and as close to the edges as possible. Backstitch at the end of your stitch line.

2 Sew three horizontal stitch lines across the 11" length of the brown wool, 2¼" apart. These will become the rows for the linen vegetables.

3 Cut three 2"-wide strips of linen along the grain of the 6" × 6" piece. Start pulling threads from the 6" sides of each strip, fringing the linen ¾" in on either side. Cut each strip across the 2" width into eight pieces of varying sizes. You now have twenty-four fringed linen pieces that will become the vegetables.

4 Line up the unfringed center section of the linen pieces along the stitched line on the brown felt, randomly spacing eight linen pieces on each garden row. Using a very small stitch (#1 on most machines), stitch down the center of the linen pieces, attaching them to the brown wool felt over the previous stitch lines. Leave a space between each small piece of linen. Backstitch at the beginning and end of each row.

5 Using a pin to help you, fringe the linen pieces all the way down to the stitch line. Trim the first row so it is about ¾" tall. For the second row, snip the fringe with the tip of your trimming scissors so they are all different lengths. For the third row, trim the fringe to stand about ⅛" tall.

6   Use the circle template and water-erasable pen to draw a 1" circle, about 1½" in from the side edge and 3" from the bottom edge. Cut out the circle with the trimming scissors.

7   Lay the light green felt onto your work surface. Center the garden right side up on top of the felt (the light green felt will be exposed slightly on all four sides), and pin the two layers together. Stitch around the edges with a ¼" seam allowance.

8   Make the fence: Using your rotary cutter, cut eighty 2" × ¼" pieces from the 2" × 20" buckram strip. These will become the fence posts.

9   On the cutting mat, lay down a piece of tape, sticky side up, the length of the mat. Place the tape about ½" above the ruled bottom line printed on the cutting mat. Tape both ends of the long tape piece to the cutting mat to hold it in place.

10   Lay the fence posts on the tape attached to your cutting mat, ¼" apart and flush with the line on the mat or the ruler. The measurements on the edge of your mat will make it easy to evenly space the fence pieces. The tape should stick to the center of all the posts so it won't get in the way when you are sewing the two buckram strips in place in Step 11. When you get close to the end of the tape, remove the small tape pieces securing the fence to the mat, slide the fence almost completely off the board, and attach a new piece of tape to the first. Continue laying out the remaining posts until you have one long strip. When you're done placing all the posts, carefully remove the taped fence-post strip from the cutting board.

11   With the sticky side of the tape facing up, stitch one of the ¼" buckram strips flush across the bottom ends of the fence posts. To form the cross brace of the fence, sew the remaining ¼" strip ½" down from the tops of the posts. Backstitch at the beginning and end of each stitch line. Remove the tape and place the fence around the garden (you can roll it up with the mat when it's not in use).

inlaid wool knit scarf *Hand-sew*

With only boiled wool jersey, scissors, and a whipstitch, you can create a bold, striking, graphic scarf. Simply wash and dry the fabric until it is felted, cut out your design, and inlay contrasting panels in the holes. Once the fabric has been shrunk down it can be cut and sewn together like felt without any hems or finished edges. You can also use this technique to inlay designs into Recycled Sweater Hats (page 50).

MATERIALS

½ yard 100% single- or double-knit wool jersey, 54" wide, for scarf body

½ yard 100% single- or double-knit wool jersey, in contrasting color for inlays

¼ yard 100% single- or double-knit wool jersey, in another contrasting color for inlays

Tracing paper, for pattern

Thread to match

Hand-sewing needle

Trimming scissors

Note: The shrinkage of wool knits varies, but you should estimate losing approximately one-third of the length of your yardage in shrinkage, as well as a lesser portion of the width. Calculate your yardage accordingly, and have extra fabric on hand if possible.

1 Wash and dry all wool jersey pieces on high heat two to three times, until well-felted. (If you are using a single-knit wool, the edges may roll after washing. The rolled edge can be trimmed off or kept as a detail. Double-knit wool tends to lie flat before and after washing.)

2 Trim a 9" strip off the width of the fabric.

3 Trace and cut out the pattern pieces using the measurements on the illustration below to recreate this design, or come up with your own. Lay the pattern pieces on the scarf and adjust until you are satisfied with the placement. Pin the pattern pieces to the scarf body.

4 Using trimming scissors, cut out all the shapes, leaving holes in the scarf.

5 Unpin the pattern pieces from the cutouts and reuse them to cut the same shapes from the contrasting fabrics, according to the illustration.

6 Lay the contrasting fabric shapes into the corresponding holes on the scarf. Attach each shape with a small whipstitch.

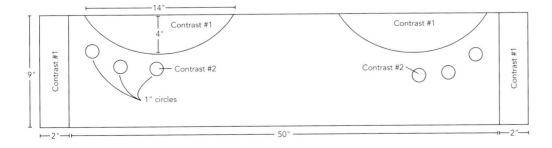

tea-dyed shawl *Hand-sew*

The sequins on this delicate silk shawl catch the light and sparkle, while the tea dye creates a soft, antique color. There is no mess when you dye fabrics with tea, and the process uses only natural materials.

MATERIALS

2 yards fine silk gauze, ends torn and slightly fringed

10 to 15 black tea bags

Large stockpot, for dyeing

Large bowl

Elastic band

Sharp or embroidery needle

Thread to match

30 to 40 silver sequins

1　Boil four quarts water in the large stockpot. Remove the paper tags from ten tea bags and tie the strings together. Add the bags to the boiling water and steep for 5 minutes, adding more tea bags or steeping longer for a darker color. Stir the water to agitate the bags so they release all of their color. Turn the heat down to a simmer and remove the tea bags.

2　Wet the silk before you place it in the tea dye. This will help the dye absorb evenly into the silk. Place the silk in the dye, stir it twice with a wooden spoon, then transfer it to the large bowl.

3　Rinse the silk under cold water and check to see if the color is to your liking. If you want a darker shade, dip the silk into the dye again and repeat the dye and rinse process.

4　Have a friend help you twist the shawl tightly until it doubles back on itself and forms a spiral. Secure the ends with an elastic band. This will give your shawl a wonderful wrinkled texture, but can take up to 48 hours to dry. Letting it hang and air dry naturally will shorten the drying time, but will not create the same wrinkled texture.

5　Stitch the sequins: Thread the needle, and knot the end of the thread. Insert the needle into the fabric to secure the knot. Make three stitches through the center of the sequin, catching the silk below with each stitch. Knot off the thread on the back of the scarf and trim it. Stitch fifteen to twenty randomly spaced sequins to each end of the shawl.

WRAPPING FABRIC GIFTS

bias blossom variations

Decorate the top of a package with a
Bias Blossom (see page 22) to give two
gifts in one! Or, follow Steps 1–4 of the
Bias Blossom instructions to make a fabric
pompom as shown below. It looks brilliant
in iridescent silk. Place the pompom on
a package or use as a holiday ornament.
To adhere blossoms or pompoms to a gift,
stitch it to the ribbon or glue it directly
onto the wrapping.

moiré ribbon

To create elegant moiré ribbon, tear narrow strips from the weft edge of moiré fabric, then pull several threads from the torn edges to create fringe.

fabric wrapping and bias ribbon

Fusible woven interfacing stiffens fabric so it can be easily wrapped around a package. This wrapping is perfect on small packages. Tie it up with some bias ribbon to complete the look.

MATERIALS

Cotton, linen, or thin wool suiting (synthetics may melt and fusible interfacing may bleed through lightweight silks)

Fusible woven interfacing

Kraft paper (optional)

Iron, ironing board, and press cloth

Fabri-Tac adhesive

Bias ribbon (see below)

To make Bias Ribbon, cut a length of bias long enough for your wrapping job (see page 131) and use it in place of ribbon. If necessary, connect more than one piece of bias to get the length you need (see page 132).

1. Cut a piece of fabric and interfacing slightly larger than the size you will need to wrap your package. (If you're not sure about the size you will need, wrap your package in kraft paper or newspaper, then measure.) Place the interfacing on an ironing board with the fusible side up. Place the fabric right side up on top of the interfacing. Place a press cloth on top and press in 10- to 20-second increments until the fabric is fused to the interfacing.

2. Wrap the fused fabric around the package to determine the final measurement. Trim the fabric to size and wrap the package as you would with wrapping paper, using Fabri-Tac adhesive rather than tape to hold it together. (Alternatively, pin the fabric wrapping in place, then secure it with ribbon and remove the pins.)

moiré gift pouch

Wrapping paper is often made to look like moiré, so why not use the real thing for wrapping a gift? To create the fringed edge of the opening on this pouch, simply tear the fabric to length in the weft direction, and cut it to width in the warp direction. The measurements below are for three nesting sizes, but you can adjust the measurements as necessary to best accommodate your gift. These pouches will only accommodate flexible fabric gifts, not boxes.

MATERIALS

Moiré fabric: 12" long (weft) × 16" wide (warp), for small pouch; 14" long (weft) × 18" wide (warp), for medium pouch; 16" long (weft) × 20" wide (warp), for large pouch

Ribbon or bias tubing (see page 133), for tie

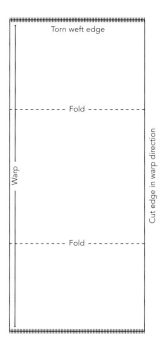

1. Create fringe by pulling several threads out from the torn weft edges until you are satisfied with the way it looks. For more information on fringing, see page 130.

2. With the right side up, fold the fringed edges in so they overlap in the center by about 2". Pin the cut ends to hold the folds in place.

3. With a ½" seam allowance, stitch the cut ends closed. Turn the pouch right side out. Fold your gift to the correct size and insert into the pouch. Use ribbon or bias tubing to tie the pouch closed.

wrapping cloths

This project was inspired by the Korean tradition of presenting gifts in elaborately patchworked wrapping cloths called *pojagi*. Generally, these cloths are the property of the gift-giver, and are reused again and again. Traditional *pojagi* are works of art in themselves, and can take many months of hand-stitching to create. You do not have to spend months stitching to carry on elements of this tradition—by following these instructions, you should be finished in under an hour. To make a larger cloth, start with larger pieces of linen and silk. Determine the correct size of the wrapping cloth for your gift by wrapping it in tissue paper first.

MATERIALS

12" × 12" piece linen, for outside
12" × 12" piece silk, for lining
40" × ⅛" fabric ribbon, for tie

Thread to match

Hand-sewing needle

Small piece paper, for label (optional)

1. Lay out the linen and silk pieces, right sides together, on your work surface and pin the edges.

2. Stitch around the square with a ½" seam allowance, leaving a 2" opening on one side for turning.

3. Turn the work, press the edges, and stitch the hole closed with a slip stitch.

4. Fold the ribbon in half. With a needle and thread, tack the center point of the ribbon in place at one of the four corners.

5. Place the gift in the center of the cloth and fold the two opposite sides without ribbon into the center. Then fold the remaining side without ribbon into the center. Fold the side with the ribbon into the center and tie the ribbon around the bundle.

6. To make a label, cut a small paper rectangle, write a message on it, and stitch it to the flap opposite the tie.

gift tags

These quick-to-make little cards are a good way to use up short pieces of leftover ribbon.

MATERIALS

Two 2" × 3½" pieces cardstock

3" fabric ribbon

Mat knife

Clear plastic ruler

Thread to match

Hand-sewing needle (optional)

2" × 3½" piece Steam-A-Seam 2 Double Stick Fusible Web

Iron, ironing board, and press cloth

Mini hole punch

Sewing machine or thread and needle for stitching ribbon in place

1. Using a mat knife and a ruler, cut a slit about ½" in from both short ends of one of the cardstock pieces. Cut the slit so it is wide enough to accommodate the ribbon.

2. Slip the ends of the ribbon through the slits so they come out the back side of the card. If desired, stitch the ends of the ribbon in place with a machine or by hand, or just leave the ends without stitching.

3. Lay the card, wrong side up, on the work surface. Peel the paper backing off of one side of the Steam-A-Seam and lay it, sticky side down, onto the card.

4. Peel the paper backing from the other side of the Steam-A-Seam and lay the remaining card piece to it, so the edges of both cards line up.

5. Transfer the card sandwich to the ironing board. Place a press cloth on top and press in 10- to 20-second increments until the two cards are fused together (do not exceed 60 seconds total); this will bond the front and back of the card together and hold the ribbon ends in place.

6. Make a small hole using a mini hole punch, tie a string through the hole, and attach the tag to your package.

VARIATION

If you would like to decorate your card with more than one piece of ribbon, cut the number of slits you need to accommodate your ribbon in Step 1. For example, if you have three pieces ¼" ribbon, then make three ¼" slits on each of the short ends of the card.

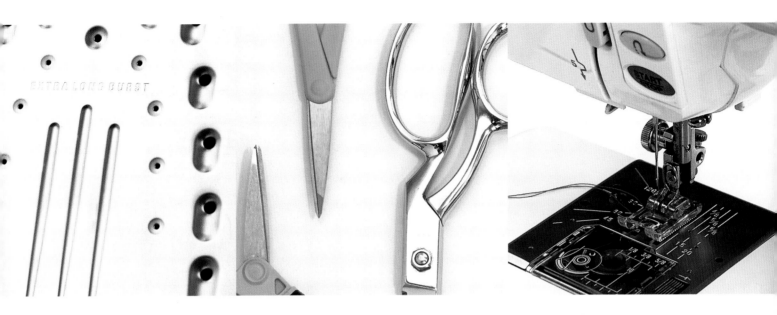

TOOLS AND TECHNIQUES

Creating with fabric has been my passion for years—I got the textile bug from my mother way back. For as long as I can remember, I have been searching out new tools and playing with fabric to come up with creative ways to construct and manipulate it. Following is an overview of the tools and techniques I find most useful and are used in the projects in this book.

tools

ROTARY CUTTING TOOLS

ROTARY CUTTER
This tool, which operates like a pizza cutter, is a favorite of mine. You can use it to cut through one or more layers of fabric and it is much faster and more accurate than scissors for straight cuts.

ROTARY CUTTING MAT
This cutting mat has measurements printed on it and is made to be used with rotary cutters as well as with mat knives. It provides a great work and cutting surface that will both protect your table top and make measuring easy and accurate.

CLEAR PLASTIC RULER
This ruler comes in many shapes, sizes, and widths, and is made from hard, clear plastic so rotary cutters will not damage it. I recommend buying one with a nonslip back.

SCISSORS

FABRIC SCISSORS
I have several different pairs of fabric scissors, but the ones I use most have spring-loaded handles. I like these because they are easier on my hands when I am doing a lot of cutting. When shopping for scissors, try a few different brands and choose a pair that feels comfortable and sturdy in your hand. In order to keep the blades sharp, it is important to use your fabric scissors only for cutting fabric.

TRIMMING SCISSORS
These small, sharp-pointed scissors come in various styles. They are less cumbersome than a full-size pair of scissors for trimming threads and provide more control for delicate jobs.

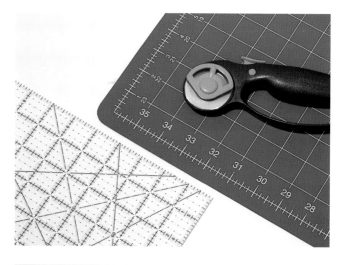

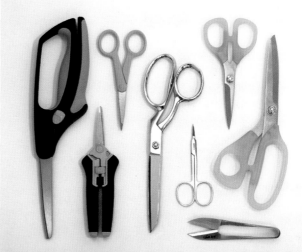

SEWING MACHINES AND ACCESSORIES

SEWING MACHINE

I come from a family of yard-salers. My mother finds a few used machines every summer and fools around with them until each one is working like a charm. She then distributes them to the sewing-machine needy and she is back on the hunt again. If you are not so handy or inclined, you can bring your yard-sale find to a professional to be serviced (we do sometimes resort to this). The drawback to yard-sale machines is that they may not include the manual or the needed accessories, but usually these can be ordered from the manufacturer.

If you want to buy a new machine, it is best to try out several models at the store and see what feels right for you. There are so many to choose from, from the most basic to the more advanced computerized, programmable quilting models. While working on this book, I approached the Janome company to learn more about their machines. The people there were kind enough to lend me a few of their home models for testing and timing the projects. I have been thrilled with them and happily recommend them.

MACHINE NEEDLES

Machine needles come in various sizes for different weights of fabric. One of the first things to check when your machine is sewing poorly (after checking the threading of the machine) is the needle itself. Check that you are using the right size needle for the fabric you are sewing and that the needle isn't damaged. If the needle is damaged, it may cause pulls in the fabric being sewn. Feel the point of the needle with your fingertip. If you feel a burr at the end of the needle, then it is time to change it.

MACHINE FEET

There are many different feet to choose from (each performing a different function), but for the projects in this book I used only two feet: a standard foot, which is used for both straight and zigzag stitching, and a zipper foot, which is narrower and allows you to stitch with the needle very close to the teeth of a zipper.

THREAD

For all of the machine sewing in this book, I used 100% polyester thread. I like this thread because it is durable and comes in hundreds of colors. If you are making a project that you want to dye, I suggest that you use white cotton thread, since polyester thread cannot be easily dyed at home.

IRONS AND ACCESSORIES

IRON

When you are buying a new iron, get the best one you can afford. Inexpensive irons can be very temperamental, sometimes getting too hot and burning your fabric, or leaking and staining it.

Here are a few tips on ironing:

- Always keep the sole plate of the iron clean so nothing from its surface transfers to your fabric.

- If you are working with an iron that tends to get too hot, test the heat on a scrap of fabric before you press the actual project.

- When using the steam feature on an iron, make sure that the iron is heated completely before pushing the steam button. If it is not fully heated, water may leak out rather than steam, leaving stains on your fabric.

- If you are working with a leaky iron, you can avoid stains by using a separate spray bottle to dampen the fabric rather than filling the iron with water and using its built-in steam or spray features.

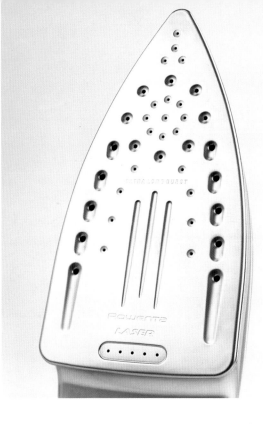

SPRAY BOTTLE

Spraying fabric with water while ironing is great for getting out tough wrinkles and making crisp, folded edges. Always test on scrap fabric first (especially on silks) to avoid water spots.

PRESS CLOTH

Whether you want to protect delicate fabrics from the iron or protect the iron from fusible adhesives, it is a good idea to have a press cloth handy. Place the press cloth on top of the fabric so there is no direct contact between the iron and the fabric. Linen makes a good press cloth because it can tolerate high heat, but cotton will work well also. Dishcloths and scraps of linen leftover from projects often make excellent press cloths.

IRON CLEANER

Keep a tube of iron cleaner handy to clean the sole plate of your iron. A dirty iron can leave hard-to-remove stains on your fabric.

MARKING TOOLS

WATER-ERASABLE MARKING PEN

The marks from this pen wipe off with a damp cloth. It can be used for embroidery designs or for making temporary marks on your fabric, such as for placement of handles or buttons.

AIR-ERASABLE MARKING PEN

Marks from this pen gradually disappear over several hours. It can be used in the same way as the water-erasable pen.

FABRIC-MARKING PENCIL

This pencil comes in a variety of colors and is good for making marks that will be hidden inside the project. Some pencils are water-soluble and will come out in the first wash and some are not. To be safe, I usually use them in places that will not be seen from the outside of the project.

PERMANENT FABRIC-MARKING PEN

Use this pen for making special tags or for signing your fabric gifts.

OTHER TOOLS

LOOP TURNER

This tool turns thin bias tubes that can be used for button loops and ties.

MEASURING TAPE

I like to use a long (120") measuring tape with inches marked on one side and centimeters on the other.

ULTRASUEDE THIMBLE

I have never been able to get used to standard metal thimbles. They are too cumbersome for me, so I make leather or Ultrasuede versions for myself that are thin and work perfectly for jobs where your finger needs a little bit of protection. To make one, place your finger down on a piece of paper and trace around the tip just beyond the first knuckle; add a ¼" seam allowance to the fingertip pattern. Cut two pattern pieces in leather or Ultrasuede and hold the pieces together with the wrong sides facing. Using a leather needle and topstitching thread (thicker than standard sewing thread and usually used for decorative topstitching), stitch together the rounded edges of the pieces with a small blanket stitch (see page 136).

PINS AND NEEDLES

Pins

STRAIGHT PINS

I like to use fine glass-head pins (.50 mm, 1³/₈" long). They do not leave marks in most fabric. They are also easy to grab and easy to find when you drop them.

PINCUSHION

I keep a dish of pins on my cutting table and a pin-cushion by my machine. It would be time-consuming to store every pin I use in a cushion, but at my machine the cushion keeps them organized as I remove them from the project as I am sewing.

Needles

As a rule, for general sewing it is best to choose a needle based on the weight of your fabric—fine, thin needles for delicate fabrics and thicker needles for heaver fabrics. Choose an eye size based on what you are threading (thread, yarn, ribbon, etc.). If your needle does not go through the fabric with ease, switch to another smaller or larger needle that does.

I like to use a piece of wool felt to keep my needles organized. Seeing their eyes and lengths helps me to choose the appropriate one for whatever I am working on at the moment without having to dig through my sewing kit. It also gives me a safe, organized place to store them when I am finished.

CHENILLE NEEDLES

These needles have sharp points and long eyes. They are traditionally used for general embroidery and sewing, ribbon embroidery, and handworked buttonholes.

COTTON DARNERS

These are long needles with sharp points and oval eyes and are commonly used for basting.

EMBROIDERY NEEDLES

These are sharp needles with long eyes and are appropriate for general sewing and embroidery.

CREWEL NEEDLES

These medium-length needles have oval eyes and are ideal for both hand embroidery and general sewing.

QUILTING BETWEENS

These small, thin needles have round eyes and sharp points and work well for quilting and detailed handwork.

GLOVERS/LEATHER NEEDLES

These are short needles with cutting, bladelike points that allow you to sew leather, fur, and suede, as well as fabrics that have leatherlike qualities.

DOLL NEEDLES

These needles are very long and are suitable for sewing dolls and other soft structures.

YARN DARNERS

These long, thick needles have large eyes and sharp points that allow you to sew with yarn.

TAPESTRY NEEDLE

These thick needles have blunt ends and very long eyes. They are often used with yarn and can easily accommodate several strands at one time. Their blunt ends slide between the fibers of fabric without splitting them. These needles are appropriate for heavy wools and tapestries. To thread a tapestry needle, fold the end of the yarn before pushing it through the eye. This will prevent the strand from splitting as you thread the needle.

SHARPS

These sharp needles are similar to embroidery needles, but have round eyes. They are appropriate for general sewing.

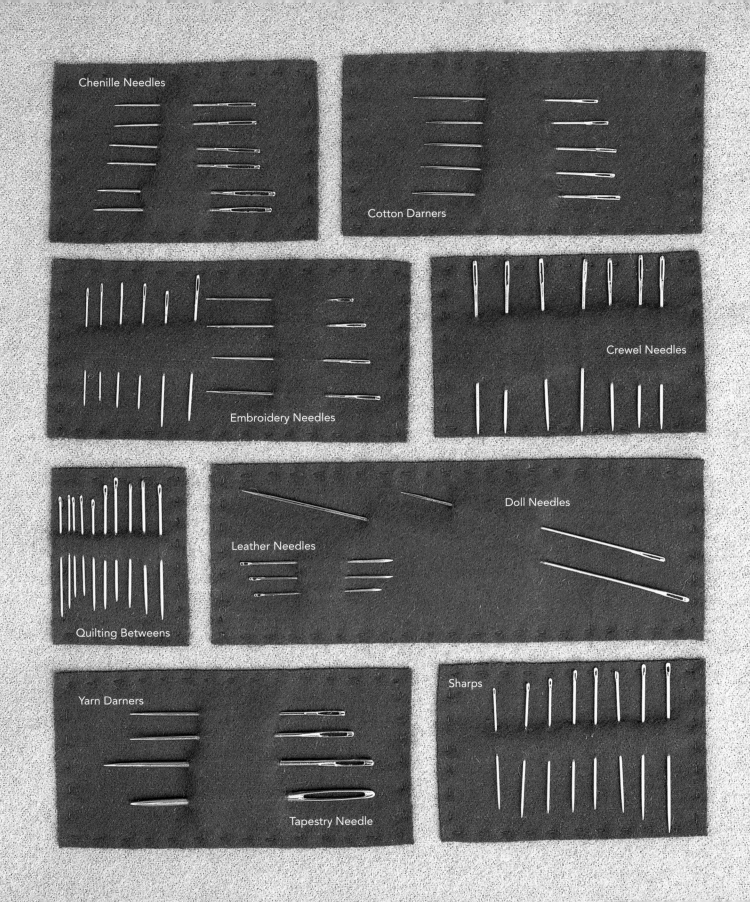

Chenille Needles

Cotton Darners

Embroidery Needles

Crewel Needles

Quilting Betweens

Leather Needles

Doll Needles

Yarn Darners

Tapestry Needle

Sharps

ADHESIVES

There are so many adhesives on the market that it is hard to sort through them all. The following list includes the adhesives I used in the projects in this book, and a few others I especially like. Before using a new adhesive, always test it first on a scrap of fabric from your project to make sure that it is appropriate for the job.

ALEENE'S ORIGINAL TACKY GLUE

A water-based latex white glue that is very thick and tacky. I first started using it over ten years ago for making architectural models. It quickly dries clear, making it perfect for that application. I use it for all sorts of things now, but especially for projects where I am attaching paper to fabric or paper to paper. Keep in mind that due to its thickness it is not easy to spread over large areas, so use it for smaller spot-gluing projects.

FABRI-TAC

This glue is clear and has a consistency similar to rubber cement, but does not need a two-sided bond. It dries so quickly that as you take its tip away from the work, strings will sometimes form as they do with hot glue. It makes a fast, strong bond on fabric-to-fabric applications, and because of its quick dry time will not bleed through most fabrics (but always test it first). It dries clear and flexible.

STEAM-A-SEAM

There are two types of this iron-fusible web, the original Steam-A-Seam sticky back and Steam-A-Seam 2. The only difference is that the original has one lightly tacky pressure-sensitive side and Steam-a-Seam 2 is tacky on both sides. The tacky surface provides a temporary and repositionable hold to your fabric so your layered pieces are easier to work with and do not shift. This product is wonderful for all sorts of no-sew projects. It forms a sturdy fabric-to-fabric or fabric-to-paper bond.

UNIQUE STITCH

This is a thick, fast-drying, machine-washable and machine-dryable fabric glue that comes in a handy tube. It makes great fabric-to-fabric bonds and is flexible when it dries. It can be used for quick-fix jobs when there is no sewing machine handy, or to hold down an edge before sewing when pins would get in the way.

FABRIC GLUE STICK

This water-soluble, acid-free adhesive in an easy-to-control stick provides an alternative to basting.

FRAY CHECK

This sealant is clear and has a thin consistency. It absorbs into the edges of your fabric and stops fibers from fraying.

WONDER TAPE

This water-soluble adhesive tape can be used as an alternative to basting. I find it particularly handy for holding zippers in place without pins.

QUILTER'S CHOICE BASTING GLUE

This glue is a good alternative to basting or pinning. The container has a very fine tip so you can lay a fine line of glue on your edge without a mess.

STIFFEN STUFF

This water-soluble stiffening spray leaves fabric with a stiff hand after it dries.

techniques

CUTTING FABRIC ON THE GRAIN

Woven fabric is made up of warp and weft threads. The warp threads run lengthwise; these are the threads attached to the loom before weaving begins. The weft threads run perpendicular to the warp; they are woven back and forth through the warp to create the fabric.

For certain projects it is necessary to cut fabric in a straight line that follows the warp or weft. This is called "cutting on the grain." To do this, cut a small (about ¼") snip in the edge of the fabric at the point where you would like to begin to cut. Starting at the snip, pull a single thread out from the weave of the fabric all the way across; this will leave a gap in the grain that can be followed to make a cut exactly on the grain line. If the thread breaks as you are pulling (which is common), cut up to where it broke, then grab hold of the same thread and continue pulling. After you have pulled the thread all the way out, finish cutting on the exposed straight grain line. Repeat the process on the remaining three sides of the fabric to cut it to the appropriate size. Now the sides of your fabric are square to the grain and ready to hem or fringe.

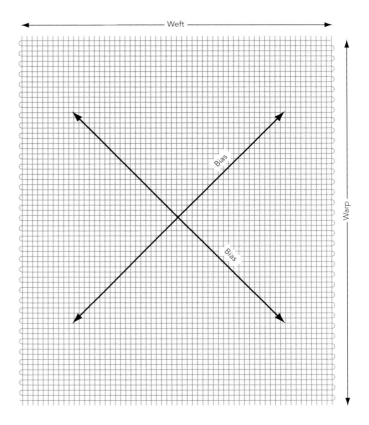

FRINGING AN EDGE

Once you have cut the edges of your fabric on the straight grain, you can easily create natural fringe. On the edge where you want fringe, make a stitch line about ½" to 1" from the edge using a very small stitch (#1 on most machines). Simply adjust the seam allowance for longer or shorter fringe. Remove any threads that are parallel to and on the outside of the stitch line to expose an even fringe.

CUTTING ON THE BIAS

Anything cut on an angle to the straight grain of the fabric is considered to be cut on the bias, but the true bias runs at a 45-degree angle to the warp and the weft. Bias strips can be used in many different ways—from encasing unfinished edges to making Bias Blossoms (see page 22) to creating tiny tubes that can be used for loops, ties, and cording. Bias strips stretch to easily turn rounded corners without buckling, and their edges fray without unraveling, allowing you to make interesting deconstructed trims. Following are instructions for cutting bias strips with a rotary cutter and with scissors. I prefer using a rotary cutter because I am able to cut strips with straighter, cleaner edges more quickly and accurately than when I cut strips with scissors. But some people prefer to use scissors, so I've included both methods.

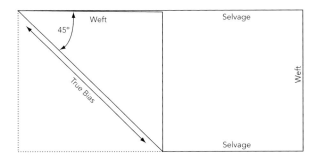

Cutting Bias Strips with a Rotary Cutter and Mat

1. Orient a rotary cutting mat on your work surface so its longest edge is parallel to the edge of the work surface.

2. Lay the fabric on the cutting mat so the selvage edge is parallel to the edge of the work surface. Fold up the lower left-hand corner so the weft edge is parallel to the top selvage edge, creating a 45-degree angle at the top left-hand corner. The fold created by this action is the true bias of the fabric.

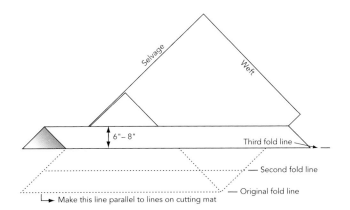

3. Rotate the fabric so the folded bias edge is parallel to one of the horizontal cutting lines on the mat. Fold up the bias edge so the fold is evenly 6" to 8" high along its length. Fold up the edge one to two more times to form a long, even roll of fabric. Adjust the bottom edge once more, aligning it with one of the lower lines on the cutting mat. Use the rotary cutter and clear plastic ruler to cut off sections (perpendicular to the true bias edge) in the width needed. Unroll the cut sections and connect them or cut them to length as necessary.

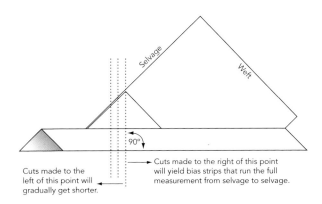

Cutting Bias Strips with Scissors

1. Lay the fabric on the work surface so the selvage edge is parallel to the edge of the work surface.

2. Use the bias length chart (see below) to help determine where to cut the fabric to achieve the length of bias needed. You can also cut several lengths of bias and connect them to create a longer strip.

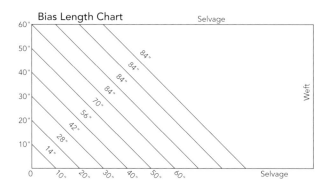

3. Use the bias length chart to achieve the length of bias necessary for your project. With a clear plastic ruler or yardstick, connect the points and mark the diagonal line (true bias) on your fabric with a fabric pencil. From this line, measure the width of the bias you need and mark another line with the fabric pencil. Mark all the lines needed for the project, then carefully cut on the lines with scissors. Connect the bias strips or cut them to length as necessary.

CONNECTING BIAS STRIPS

Sometimes you have to connect two or more pieces of bias in order to get the length you need. Here's an easy way to do it, sewing on the grain for secure stitches that won't fall apart.

1. Lay the end of one bias strip right side up and horizontal to the work surface. Place the end of the other piece right side down and vertically on top of the first piece, with the ends overlapping. Pin the overlapped fabric. Using a very small stitch (#1 on most machines), stitch from point A to point B (see below).

2. Trim off the crossed ends, leaving a ⅛" seam allowance.

3. Continue to connect strip ends in this manner until you have the length you need for your project.

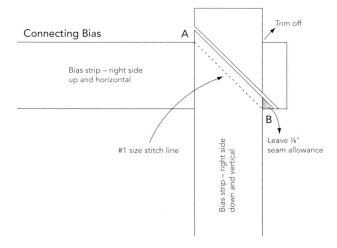

CREATING BIAS TUBES

Also known as fabric spaghetti, bias tubes have many applications, including making loops, buttonholes, Chinese frog closures, and drawstrings. These thin tubes are made by sewing bias strips in half lengthwise and then, using a special tool called a tube turner, turning the strips right side out.

1. Cut a 1¼"-wide bias strip (or whatever width is required for the project). Connect the bias strips or cut them to length as necessary.

2. Fold the end of the bias strip in half lengthwise and pinch the end to hold the fold.

3. Place the pinched end under the foot of your machine and lower the needle down into the fabric at the center point of the folded strip. Stretch the folded strip as you stitch down its centerline. The stretching is very important because when you turn the tube right side out it will need to expand to accommodate the seam allowance within it. If you do not stretch the fabric while sewing, the thread may break during the turning process and the finished tube may not have the stretch it needs for most applications.

4. To turn the tube right side out, insert the hook end of a tube turner into the tube until it comes out at the opposite end.

5. Poke the hook's latch through the fabric close to the end of the tube on the fold line, then pull the hooked end of the tube into the tube itself, until the hook exits the other end and the tube is right side out. Different weights of fabric will turn with various degrees of ease or difficulty (thin, slippery fabrics tend to be the easiest to turn; heavy fabrics can be challenging). As you are turning, be aware that the hook's hold may be tenuous, so pull it through gingerly without backing the hook up at all. Backing up will release the hook midturn and it is very difficult to reattach at that point.

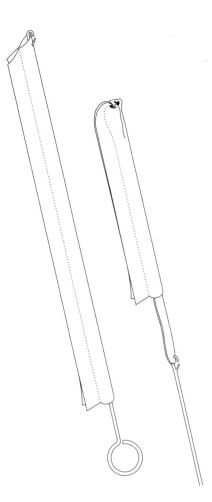

SETTING A SIMPLE ZIPPER
FOR AN 18" PILLOW

For the Patchwork Pillow (page 62) and the Red Cross
Appliquéd Pillow (page 64), I give two closure options—
either no special closure, meaning that the cover can
only be removed by unstitching, or a zippered closure.
Here are the instructions for making a pillow with a
zipper. For a full, fluffy-looking pillow, finish your pillow
cover 1" smaller than your pillow filling. You can achieve
this by cutting your fabric to the same size as the finished
filling and allowing yourself a ½" seam allowance all
the way around.

MATERIALS

18" × 18" piece fabric, for front

16½" × 18" piece fabric and 2½" × 18"
piece fabric, for back

22" polyester all-purpose zipper

Thread to match

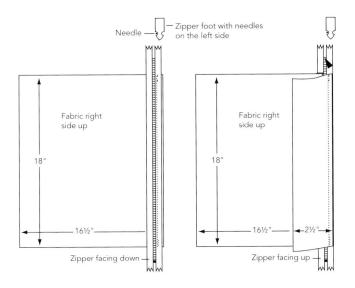

1. Lay the zipper, closed and face down, along one of the
   18" sides of the 16½" × 18" fabric piece (fabric should
   be right side up). The zipper ends will overhang the
   edges of the fabric by about 2". Match the zipper tape
   edge and the fabric edge to one another and pin the
   zipper in place.

2. Using a zipper foot, stitch along the zipper tape with
   the side of the foot resting against the teeth as you
   stitch (about ⅜" seam allowance). Because of the
   zipper's extra length, the zipper pull should be out of
   your way the entire time you are sewing, so there is no
   need to open and close the zipper as you sew.

3. Splay the zipper and the fabric open so their right
   sides are facing up. Lay the 18" edge of the 2½" strip
   face down onto the unsewn side of the zipper tape.
   Pin the fabric to the zipper tape, aligning the edges.

4. Using the zipper foot, stitch along the fabric edge
   (with the zipper facing up under the fabric) close
   to the zipper's teeth, as in Step 2.

5. Splay the fabric open to expose the zipper and
   press flat. Unzip the zipper partway so you will be
   able to turn the pillow after the front and back are
   stitched together.

6. With right sides of the front and back together, align
   all the edges and pin them. Sew around the edges
   of the square with a ½" seam allowance, backstitching
   over both ends of the zipper to secure them. Trim
   off the overhanging zipper ends.

7. Turn the pillow cover right side out, press it, and stuff
   it with the pillow filling.

THREADING A HAND-SEWING NEEDLE

Cut a piece of thread approximately 30" long. Longer pieces are more likely to weaken, tangle, or break during the sewing process. Thread the needle using the end of the thread as it comes off of the spool, the same end you would use to thread your machine. If you thread your needle with the freshly cut end, it will twist and tangle. The thread is spun and wound onto the spool to go through your machine in one direction without tangling. You will run into fewer tangles when hand-sewing if you follow the thread's natural twist.

STITCHING

Basting

By basting a seam you can quickly prepare it to be machine- or hand-sewn. Basting will hold the seam in place without pins, which can be cumbersome in some applications. To create a basting stitch, simply lengthen a running stitch to approximately ½" or longer to allow for easy removal of the thread once you have completed your permanent stitches.

Tacking Stitch

A tacking stitch is used to secure a single point.

1. Secure the thread in the work with a knot.

2. Make several small stitches on top of one another until the point feels secure.

Blanket Stitch

Use a blanket stitch as a decorative way to finish an edge.

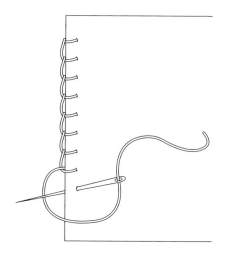

1. With a clear plastic ruler and a water-erasable pen, mark a line approximately ¼" in from the edge of your work to use as a guide for your stitches (this measurement can be changed to fit various applications). Once you master this stitch, you probably won't need to create this line to follow.

2. Hold the edge of the work vertically and right side up.

3. Secure the thread in the work with a knot.

4. Insert the needle horizontally into the work (front to back) at the premarked line.

5. Place the thread behind the needle's point and pull the needle through so the thread is taut against the fabric edge. Do not pull it so taut that the fabric bunches.

6. Continue inserting the needle, placing the thread behind the needle tip, and pulling taut until the edge is complete.

Fell Stitch

Use a fell stitch to join a folded edge to a base fabric from the right side; for example, stitching down appliqué pieces or attaching a bias-bound edge, as in this illustration.

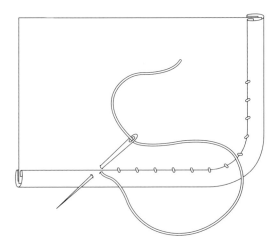

1. Secure the thread in the work with a knot on the inside of the folded edge to be stitched down. Exit your needle at the fold.

2. Insert the needle into the base fabric opposite where it came out of the folded edge. Bring the needle point up through the bottom of the work at approximately 1/8" forward so it just catches the folded edge.

3. Continue inserting and exiting the needle in this manner, just catching the folded edge of the piece to be attached.

Note: If you are working this stitch on a folded bias trim, do not go through all the layers of fabric. This way your stitch will be invisible on the opposite side and minimal from the side you work it on. In an application where the back of the stitch is on the inside of the work (for example, an appliquéd patch) the stitch on the back will have a diagonal appearance.

Running Stitch

A running stitch can be used for many applications. It is not a particularly strong stitch so I generally use it as a decorative detail or on seams that will not be stressed (for example, topstitching the trimmed edge on the Silk-Trimmed Wool Blanket on page 72). The size of the running stitch can vary depending on the desired appearance, thickness of the fabric, or application. On thick wools you may not be able to make as delicate a stitch (if you go through the entire thickness of the fabric) as on a fine silk or cotton. You may also make a purely decorative running stitch with embroidery floss to achieve a bold, colorful stitch line.

1. Secure the thread in the work with a knot.

2. Make two to three 1/8" stitches on your needle at a time, then pull the needle through the fabric.

3. Repeat this process until the work is complete.

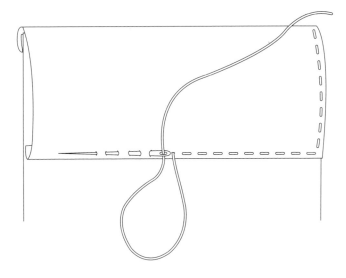

Slipstitch

Use a slipstitch to join a seam from the right side of the fabric. This stitch is basically a running stitch that is worked from the right side of the fabric and hidden on the back. It is useful when closing a hole in a seam line after turning the project right side out (as in the Barkcloth Baby Bib on page 44).

1. Secure the thread in the work with a knot on the back side of the fabric. Exit the needle on the front of the fabric on the seam line fold.

2. Insert the needle into the seam line fold directly opposite where it came out, then exit the needle about 1/8" forward.

3. Insert the needle back into the first side directly opposite where it came out and exit the needle about 1/8" forward.

4. Continue in this manner until the seam is complete, securing your thread with a knot on the back side at the end.

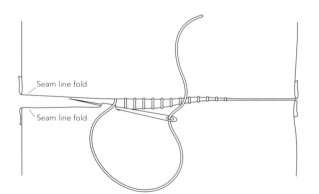

Seam line fold

Seam line fold

Whipstitch

A whipstitch can be used to decorate edges (similar to the blanket stitch), to join edges, and to make narrow seams.

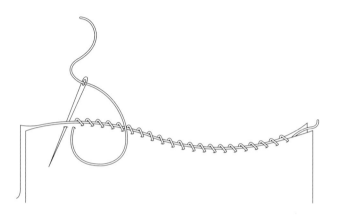

1. Secure the thread in the work with a knot. If the whipstitch will be visible on the outside of the project, secure the knot on the inside and exit the needle on the outside where you want to begin the stitch. You can work this stitch from left to right or right to left.

2. Insert the needle from the back of the seam edge to the front, inserting the needle about 1/8" in from the edge with the needle pointing toward you.

3. Pull the needle out of the front, then insert it into the back again, wrapping it around the seam edge.

4. Continue this back-to-front wrapping with about 1/8" between stitches, or whatever distance is appropriate to the project.

recommended reading

SEWING

Sew Any Fabric: A Quick Reference to Fabrics from A to Z, Claire Shaeffer (Krause Publications)

Sewing 101: A Beginner's Guide to Sewing (Creative Publishing International)

Sewing for Dummies, Janice Saunders Maresh (Wiley)

More Fabric Savvy: A Quick Resource Guide to Selecting and Sewing Fabric, Sandra Betzina (The Taunton Press)

The Complete Photo Guide to Sewing (Creative Publishing International)

All About Machine Arts: Decorative Techniques from A to Z (C&T Publishing)

INSPIRATION

World Textiles: A Visual Guide to Traditional Techniques, John Gillow and Bryan Sentance (Thames & Hudson)

Women's Work: Textile Art from the Bauhaus, Sigrid Weltge-Wortmann (Chronicle Books)

Dress in Detail from Around the World, Rosemary Crill, Jennifer Wearden, and Verity Wilson (Victoria & Albert Museum)

Twentieth-Century Pattern Design: Textile and Wallpaper Pioneers, Lesley Jackson (Princeton Architectural Press)

Gee's Bend: The Women and Their Quilts, John Beardsley, William Arnett, Paul Arnett, and Jane Livingston (Tinwood Books)

HOW-TO

Simply Felt: 20 Easy and Elegant Designs in Wool, Margaret Docherty and Jayne Emerson (Interweave Press)

White on White: Elegant Designs to Stitch, Janet Haigh (Interweave Press)

Color on Color: Elegant Designs to Stitch, Janet Haigh (Interweave Press)

The Art of Manipulating Fabric, Colette Wolff (Krause Publications)

Memory on Cloth: Shibori Now, Yoshiko Iwamoto Wada (Kodansha International)

Dyes and Paints: A Hands-On Guide to Coloring Fabric, Elin Noble (self-published, previously published by Martingale & Company)

MAGAZINES

Selvedge www.selvedge.org
PieceWork www.interweave.com
Fiberarts www.fiberarts.com
Threads www.threadsmagazine.com

sources for supplies

The following companies are good sources for the materials you will need when you are making the projects in this book, and for other general supplies. When I began this book, I contacted companies whose products I use regularly to ask questions and learn more about them. I got a warm response from all and want to thank them for their kindness, donations, and discounts, all of which helped me so much. Those companies are marked with an asterisk.

FABRICS AND TRIMMINGS

B&J FABRICS
525 7th Ave., 2nd Floor
New York, NY 10018
212 354 8150
www.bandjfabrics.com

BANKSVILLE DESIGNER FABRICS
115 New Canaan Ave.
Norwalk, CT 06850
203 846 1333
www.banksvilledesignerfabrics.com

BUTTERFLY FABRIC, INC.
Iridescent silk taffeta
260 W. 39th St.
New York, NY 10018
212 768 3940
www.butterflyfabrics.com

*J & O FABRIC CENTER
Extensive selection of discounted
fabrics, including large selection
of bark cloth patterns
9401 Rt. 130
Pennsauken, NJ 08110
856 663 2121
www.jandofabrics.com

*M&J TRIMMING
Fashion trims, ribbons, buttons, belt
buckles, etc. (over 100,000 different
items in stock)
1008 6th Ave.
New York, NY 10018
800 9 MJTRIM, 212 204 9595
www.mjtrim.com

*MASTERSTROKE CANADA
New and vintage ribbons
1766 Midland Ave.
Toronto, Canada M1P 3C2
866 249 7677, 416 751 4193
www.masterstrokecanada.com

MOOD, INC. DESIGNER FABRIC
255 W. 37th St., 3rd Floor
New York, NY 10018
212 730 5003
www.moodfabrics.com

*NEARSEA NATURALS, INC.
Certified-organic cotton fabrics
PO Box 345
Rowe, NM 87562
877 573 2913
www.nearseanaturals.com

THE SILK TRADING CO.
Silks and drapery fabric
Check website for a store
in your area
888 SILK 302, 212 966 5464
www.silktrading.com

TRIMFABRIC
PO Box 546
Gloversville, NY 12078
800 808 7995, 518 835 2079
www.trimfabric.com

TOOLS AND NOTIONS

AURORA SILK
Silk thread
5806 N. Vancouver Ave.
Portland, OR 97217
503 286 4149
www.aurorasilk.com

*FISKARS BRANDS, INC.
Cutting and crafting tools
3537 Daniels St.
Madison, WI 53718
866 348 5661
www.fiskarscrafts.com

*JANOME AMERICA, INC.
Sewing machines and accessories
10 Industrial Ave.
Mahwah, NJ 07430
201 825 3200
www.janome.com

* PRYM CONSUMER USA, INC.
Collins, Dritz, and Omnigrid notions
and cutting tools
PO Box 5028
Spartanburg, SC 29304
800 255 7796
www.dritz.com

* ROWENTA INC.
Irons, steamers, and ironing boards
196 Boston Ave.
Medford, MA 02155
781 396 0600
www.rowentausa.com

*SIGNATURE CRAFTS
Fabric and craft glues
125 MacQueston Parkway South
Mt. Vernon, NY 10550
800 865 7238
www.beaconcreates.com
www.signaturecrafts.com

STEINLAUF AND STOLLER INC.
Sewing notions
239 West 39th St.
New York, NY 10018
877 869 0321, 212 869 0321
www.steinlaufandstoller.com

PAPER

KATE'S PAPERIE
561 Broadway
New York, NY 10012
800 809 9880
www.katespaperie.com

PAPER SOURCE
Check website for a store
in your area
888 PAPER 11
ww.paper-source.com

FIGMENTS
717 Westminster St.
Providence, RI 02903
401 588 5180
www.figmentsdesign.com

**WOOL FIBER,
YARN, AND FELT**

*MARR HAVEN WOOL FARM
Premium wool and related products
for felters, knitters, crocheters,
weavers, and other fiber artists
772 39th St.
Allegan, MI 49010-9353
269 673 8800
www.marrhaven.com

PURL
Yarn and knitting supplies
137 Sullivan St.
New York, NY 10012
212 420 8796
www.purlsoho.com

A STITCH ABOVE
Yarn and knitting supplies
190 Wayland Ave.
Providence, RI 02906
800 949 KNIT, 401 455 0269
www.astitchaboveknitting.com

*THE WARM COMPANY
Products for quilting, sewing, and
crafting, including Steam-A-Seam
iron-fusible web and Warm & Natural
needled cotton quilt batting
954 E. Union St.
Seattle, WA, 98122
800 234 WARM, 206 320 9276
www.warmcompany.com

*WOOLY COMFORTS
Premium wool roving, batting,
felt, and related items
Box 2038
Chillicothe, OH 45601
740 775 1916
www.woolycomforts.com

WEIR DOLLS AND CRAFTS
Wool felt
2909 Parkridge Dr.
Ann Arbor, MI 48103-1734
888 205 5034, 734 668 6992
www.weirdolls.com

index

acknowledgments

I am fortunate to have many wonderful people in my life who have helped to make this book a reality. It all began with my dear friend Lenore Welby, who recommended me to Melanie Falick at Stewart, Tabori & Chang. Without Lenore and Melanie I never would have thought to write a book at all, but here I am one year later thanking them and so many others for their support and artistic contributions.

Melanie has been great to work with, guiding me through "first-book syndrome" and answering question after question along the way. She helped me simplify and express my ideas in a more eloquent and organized way than I could have ever done on my own.

I would also like to thank Joelle Hoverson. Her book *Last-Minute Knitted Gifts* was an inspiration, and helped me so much as I visualized its sister, *Last-Minute Fabric Gifts*.

I was so pleased that STC allowed me to choose my very talented friends and colleagues to collaborate with me on this project. Thank you Karen, for all of your gorgeous photographs. Your patience and nuanced understanding of light and composition continuously thrill me, as does your presence in my life. I am looking forward to the future. Caroline Woodward—you, my friend, helped me keep my sanity! Thank you for your organization and beautiful photostyling. And Winsor Pop, many thanks...you pulled all of the elements together into this beautifully designed book. Thank you all so very much!

Natalia Karoway-Waterhouse and Adriana Young graciously took time out to help me to test and time all of the projects, and Gillian Kiely saved me at the very end with the perfect trade. Stacy Cristo's Tie Pouch and Coat Sleeve Bag ideas are so much fun; I am so glad she agreed to let me include them. (Stacy can be reached by e-mail at stacy@seedpods.org.) Many thanks to Philip May, who supplied me with a stack of his beautiful jacquard fabrics to play with, which I used for the striped Fabric Belt. (Philip can be reached at philip@lamills.net.)

To all the friends who generously took time out to model, thank you, thank you, thank you: Alexis Lint; Zachary Miller; Caroline and Ruby Woodward; Debbie, Sam, and Alex Shirley; Natasha Harrison; Carin Wagner; Avery Slone; John and Jeremy Woodward; Jama Calgiano; Luke, Coco, and Sacha Mandle; Adriana Young; Sylvan Medyesy; and Diane Horton's kitties, who were on call for weeks awaiting their big day.

How can I thank Susan Dando, who invited us into her beautiful home, which we turned upside down for nearly a week of shooting! Debra Delgado and Warren Simmons, Hank Gilpin, Karen Philippi, Zachary Miller, and Bob Zuk also graciously opened their homes to us as shooting locations.

I would also like to thank Elizabeth Searl at Rogers & Goffigon for supplying the beautiful linen used for the Twig Handle Tote. To find out more about their sumptuous decorator fabrics, contact them at 203 532 8068.

I must offer my final thanks to my parents for the wonderful R&R intervention this spring—what a lifesaver!